# Sampling Vegetation Attributes
## Interagency Technical Reference

Cooperative Extension Service

## U.S. Department of Agriculture
— Forest Service —

Natural Resource Conservation Service,
Grazing Land Technology Institute

## U.S. Department of the Interior
— Bureau of Land Management —

1996
*Revised in 1997, and 1999*

Supersedes BLM Technical Reference 4400-4, *Trend Studies*, dated May 1985

Edited, designed, and produced by the Bureau of Land Management's
National Applied Resource Sciences Center

BLM/RS/ST-96/002+1730

# SAMPLING VEGETATION ATTRIBUTES
## Interagency Technical Reference

By (In alphabetical order)

**Bill Coulloudon**
Rangeland Management Spec.
Bureau of Land Management
Phoenix, Arizona

**Kris Eshelman** (deceased)
Rangeland Management Spec.
Bureau of Land Management
Reno, Nevada

**James Gianola**
Wildhorse and Burro Spec.
Bureau of Land Management
Carson City, Nevada

**Ned Habich**
Rangeland Management Spec.
Bureau of Land Management
Denver Colorado

**Lee Hughes**
Ecologist
Bureau of Land Management
St. George, Utah

**Curt Johnson**
Rangeland Management Spec.
Forest Service Region 4
Ogden Utah

**Mike Pellant**
Rangeland Ecologist
Bureau of Land Management
Boise, Idaho

**Paul Podborny**
Wildlife Biologist
Bureau of Land Management
Ely, Nevada

**Allen Rasmussen**
Rangeland Management Spec.
Cooperative Extension Service
Utah State University
Logan, UT

**Ben Robles**
Wildlife Biologist
Bureau of Land Management
Safford, Arizona

**Pat Shaver**
Natural Resource Conservation Service
Rangeland Management Spec.
Corvallis, Oregon

**John Spehar**
Rangeland Management Spec.
Bureau of Land Management
Rawlins, Wyoming

**John Willoughby**
State Biologist
Bureau of Land Management
Sacramento, California

Technical Reference 1734-4
copies available from
Bureau of Land Management
National Business Center
BC-650B
P.O. Box 25047
Denver, Colorado 80225-0047

# TABLE OF CONTENTS

# TABLE OF CONTENTS (continued)

# DEDICATION

This publication is dedicated to the memory of Kristen R. Eshelman, who contributed tremendously to its development and preparation. Throughout his career, Kris was instrumental in producing numerous technical references outlining procedures for rangeland inventory, monitoring, and the evaluation of rangeland data. Through his efforts, resource specialists were provided with the tools to improve the public rangelands for the benefit of rangeland users and the American public.

# I. PREFACE

The intent of this interagency monitoring guide is to provide the basis for consistent, uniform, and standard vegetation attribute sampling that is economical, repeatable, statistically reliable, and technically adequate. While this guide is not all inclusive, it does include the primary sampling methods used across the West. An omission of a particular sampling method does not mean that the method is not valid in specific locations; it simply means that it is not widely used or recognized throughout the western states. (See Section V.N, Other Methods.)

Proper use and management of our rangeland resources has created a demand for uniformity and consistency in rangeland health measurement methods. As a result of this interest, the USDI Bureau of Land Management (BLM) and USDA Forest Service met in late 1992 and agreed to establish an interagency technical team to jointly oversee the development and publishing of vegetation sampling field guides.

The 13-member team currently includes representatives from the Forest Service, BLM, the Grazing Land Technology Institute of the Natural Resource Conservation Service (NRCS), and the Cooperative Extension Service.

The interagency technical team first met in January 1994 to evaluate the existing rangeland monitoring techniques described in BLM's *Trend Studies, Technical Reference TR 4400-4*. The team spent 2 years reviewing, modifying, adding to, and eliminating techniques for this interagency *Sampling Vegetation Attributes* technical reference. Feedback from numerous reviewers, including field personnel, resulted in further refinements.

# II. INTRODUCTION

Identifying the appropriate sampling technique first requires the identification of the proper vegetation characteristic or attribute to measure. To do this the examiner must consider objectives, life form (grass, forb, shrub, or tree), distribution patterns of individuals of a species, distribution patterns between species (community mosaic pattern), efficiency of data collection from an economic standpoint, and accuracy and precision of the data.

Permittees, lessees, other rangeland users, and interested publics should be consulted and encouraged to participate in the collection and analysis of monitoring data. Those individuals or groups interested in helping to collect data should be trained in the technique used in the specific management unit.

This document deals with the collection of vegetation data. The interpretation of that data will be addressed in other documents. This document does not address interpreting vegetation data for adjusting livestock numbers or making other management decisions.

## A. Terms and Concepts
The following terms require an expanded discussion beyond the scope of the Glossary of Terms:

1. *Inventory* Inventory is the systematic acquisition and analysis of information needed to describe, characterize, or quantify vegetation. As might be expected, data for many different vegetation attributes can be collected. Inventories can be used not only for mapping and describing ecological sites, but also for determining ecological status, assessing the distribution and abundance of species, and establishing baseline data for monitoring studies.

2. *Population* A population (used here in the statistical, not the biological, sense) is a complete collection of objects (usually called units) about which one wishes to make statistical inferences. Population units can be individual plants, points, plots, quadrats, or transects.

3. *Sampling Unit* A sampling unit is one of a set of objects in a sample that is drawn to make inferences about a population of those same objects. A collection of sampling units is a sample. Sampling units can be individual plants, points, plots, quadrats, or transects.

4. *Sample* A sample is a set of units selected from a population used to estimate something about the population (statisticians call this making *inference* about the population). In order to properly make inferences about the population, the units must be selected using some random procedure (see Technical Reference, *Measuring & Monitoring Plant Populations*). The units selected are called sampling units.

5. *Sampling* Sampling is a means by which inferences about a plant community can be made based on information from an examination of a small proportion of that community. The most complete way to determine the characteristics of a population is to conduct a complete enumeration or census. In a census, each individual unit in the population is sampled to provide the data for the aggregate. This process is both time-consuming and costly. It may also result in inaccurate

values when individual sampling units are difficult to identify. Therefore, the best way to collect vegetation data is to sample a small subset of the population. If the population is uniform, sampling can be conducted anywhere in the population. However, most vegetation populations are not uniform. It is important that data be collected so that the sample represents the entire population. Sample design is an important consideration in collecting representative data. (See Section III.)

6. *Shrub Characterization* Shrub characterization is addressed here since it is not covered in most of the techniques in this technical reference. Shrub characterization is the collection of data on the shrub and tree component of a vegetation community. Attributes that could be important for shrub characterization are height, volume, foliage density, crown diameter, form class, age class, and total number of plants by species (density). Another important feature of shrub characterization is the collection of data on a vertical as well as a horizontal plane. Canopy layering is also important. The occurrence of individual species and the extent of canopy cover of each species is recorded in layers. The number of layers chosen should represent the herbaceous layer, the shrub layer, and the tree layer, though additional layers can be added if needed.

7. *Trend* Trend refers to the direction of change. Vegetation data are collected at different points in time on the same site and the results are then compared to detect a change. Trend is described as moving "towards meeting objectives," "away from meeting objectives," "not apparent," or "static." Trend data are important in determining the effectiveness of on-the-ground management actions. Trend data indicate whether the rangeland is moving towards or away from specific objectives. The trend of a rangeland area may be judged by noting changes in vegetation attributes such as species composition, density, cover, production, and frequency. Trend data, along with actual use, authorized use, estimated use, utilization, climate, and other relevant data, are considered in evaluating activity plans.

8. *Vegetation Attributes* Vegetation attributes are quantitative features or characteristics of vegetation that describe how many, how much, or what kind of plant species are present. The most commonly used attributes are:

| | |
|---|---|
| Frequency | Production |
| Cover | Structure |
| Density | Species Composition |

## B.  Techniques Not Addressed The following are not included in this document:

- Riparian Monitoring
- Monitoring Using Aerial Photography
- Special Status Plant Monitoring
- Weight Estimate and Ocular Reconnaissance Methods
- Soil Vegetation Inventory Method
- Community Structure Analysis Method
- Photo Plot Method

C. Guidelines *The techniques described here are guides for establishing and sampling vegetation attributes. They are not standards.* Vegetation sampling techniques and standards need to be based on management objectives. Techniques can be modified or adjusted to fit specific resource situations or management objectives as long as the principles of the technique are maintained. Before a modified technique is used, it should be reviewed by agency monitoring coordinators, cooperators, and other qualified individuals. A modified technique should be clearly identified and labeled as "MODIFIED." All modifications such as changes in quadrat size or transect layout should be clearly documented each time the method is used.

D. Location of Study Sites *Proper selection of study sites is critical to the* success of a monitoring program. Errors in making these selections can result in irrelevant data and inappropriate management decisions.

The site selection process used should be documented. Documentation should include the management objectives, the criteria used for selecting the sites, and the kinds of comparisons or interpretations expected to be made from them.

Common locations for studies include critical areas and key areas. Some of the site characteristics and other information that may be considered in the selection of study sites are:

- Soil
- Vegetation (kinds and distribution of plants)
- Ecological sites
- Seral stage
- Topography
- Location of water, fences, and natural barriers
- Size of pasture
- Kind and/or class of forage animals—livestock, wildlife, wild horses, and wild burros
- Habits of the animals, including foraging
- Areas of animal concentration
- Location and extent of critical areas
- Erosion conditions
- Threatened, endangered, and sensitive species—both plant and animal
- Periods of animal use
- Grazing history
- Location of salt, mineral, and protein supplements
- Location of livestock, wildlife, wild horse, and/or wild burro trails

1. *Critical Area* Critical areas are areas that should be evaluated separately from the remainder of a management unit because they contain special or unique values. Critical areas could include fragile watersheds, sage grouse nesting grounds, riparian areas, areas of critical environmental concern, etc.

2. *Key Areas* Key areas are indicator areas that are able to reflect what is happening on a larger area as a result of on-the-ground management actions. A key area should be a representative sample of a large stratum, such as a pasture, grazing allotment, wildlife habitat area, herd management area, watershed area, etc., depending on the management objectives being addressed by the study. Key areas

represent the "pulse" of the rangeland. Proper selection of key areas requires appropriate stratification. Statistical inference can only be applied to the stratification unit.

a **Selecting Key Areas** The most important factors to consider when selecting key areas are the management objectives found in land use plans, coordinated resource management plans, and/or activity plans. An interdisciplinary team should be used to select these areas. In addition, permittees, lessees, and other interested publics should be invited to participate, as appropriate, in selecting key areas. Poor information resulting from improper selection of key areas leads to misguided decisions and improper management.

b **Criteria for Selecting Key Areas** The following are some criteria that should be considered in selecting key areas. A key area:

- Should be representative of the stratum in which it is located.
- Should be located within a single ecological site and plant community.
- Should contain the key species where the key species concept is used.
- Should be capable of and likely to show a response to management actions. This response should be indicative of the response that is occurring on the stratum.

c **Number of Key Areas** The number of key areas selected to represent a stratum ideally depends on the size of the stratum and on data needs. However, the number of areas may ultimately be limited by funding and personnel constraints.

d **Objectives** Objectives should be developed so that they are specific to the key area. Monitoring studies can then be designed to determine if these objectives are being met.

e **Mapping Key Areas** Key areas should be accurately delineated on aerial photos and/or maps. Mapping of key areas will provide a permanent record of their location.

## E. Key Species

Key species are generally an important component of a plant community. Key species serve as indicators of change and may or may not be forage species. More than one key species may be selected for a stratum, depending on objectives and data needs. In some cases, problem plants (poisonous, etc.) may be selected as key species. Key species may change from season to season.

The process used to select key species should be documented. Documentation should include the management objectives, the criteria used for selecting species, and the kinds of comparisons or interpretations expected to be made from them.

a **Selecting Key Species** Selection of key species should be tied directly to objectives in land-use plans, coordinated resource management plans, and activity plans. This selection depends upon the plant species in the present plant community, the present ecological status, and the potential natural communities for the specific sites. An interdisciplinary team should be used in selecting key species to ensure that data needs of the various resources are met. In addition, interested publics should be invited to participate, as appropriate, in selecting these species (see Section II.G).

b **Considerations in Selecting Key Species** The following points should be considered in selecting key species:

- Changes in density, frequency, reproduction, etc., of key species on key areas are assumed to reflect changes in these species on the entire stratum.

- The forage value of key species may be of secondary or no importance. For example, watershed protection may require selection of plants as key species which protect the watershed but are not the best forage species. In some cases, threatened, endangered, or sensitive species that have no particular forage value may be selected as key species.

- Any foraging use of the key species on key areas is assumed to reflect foraging use of that species on the entire stratum.

- Depending on the selected management strategy and/or periods of use, key species may be foraged during the growing period, after maturity, or both.

- In areas of yearlong grazing use and in areas where there is more than one use period, several key species may be selected to sample. For example, on an area with both spring and summer grazing use, a cool season plant may be the key species during the spring, while a warm season plant may be the key species during the summer.

- Selection of several key species may be desirable when adjustments in livestock grazing use are anticipated. This is especially true if more than one plant species contributes a major portion of the forage base of the animals using the area (Smith 1965).

c. **Key Species on Depleted Rangelands** The key species selected should be present on each key area on which monitoring studies are conducted; however, on depleted rangelands these species may be sparse or absent. In this situation it may be necessary to conduct monitoring studies on other species. Data gathered on non-key species must be interpreted on the basis of effects on the establishment and subsequent response of the key species. It should also be verified that the site is ecologically capable of producing the key species.

# F.   General Observations General observations can be important when conducting evaluations of grazing allotments, wildlife habitat areas, wild horse and burro herd management areas, watershed areas, or other designated management areas. Such factors as rodent use, insect infestations, animal concentrations, fire, vandalism, and other uses of the sites can have considerable impact on vegetation and soil resources. This information is recorded on the reverse side of the study method forms or on separate pages, as necessary.

G. Coordination  Monitoring programs will be coordinated with interested publics and other appropriate state and federal agencies. Monitoring should be planned and implemented on an interdisciplinary basis.

H. Electronic Data Recorders  Electronic data recorders are handheld "computers" that are constructed to withstand the harsh environmental conditions found in the field. They are used to record monitoring data in a digital format that can be transferred directly to a personal computer for storage and retrieval. They require minimal maintenance, are generally programmable, and allow easy data entry using a wand and bar codes.

Recording field data using an electronic data recorder takes approximately the same amount of time as using printed forms. The advantage with electronic data recorders is that they improve the efficiency by reducing errors associated with entering data into a computer for analysis. They can also reduce the time needed for data compilation and summarization.

The cost of electronic data recorders and computer software programs is considerable and should be evaluated prior to purchase. It is also important to have good computer support assistance available to assist users in operating, downloading, and troubleshooting electronic data recorders, especially during the initial use period.

I. Reference Areas  Reference areas are rangelands where natural biological and physical processes are functioning normally. Reference areas serve as benchmarks for comparing management actions on rangelands. Reference areas differ from key areas in that they represents rangeland where impacts are minimal. Reference areas are found in grazing exclosures, natural areas, or areas that receive minimal grazing impacts.

Reference areas should be included in any monitoring program to evaluate the influences of natural variables (especially climate) on vegetation. Cause-and-effect relationships are better determined if the effects of climate on vegetation can be separated from management effects. Monitoring studies, especially trend studies, should therefore be established both on key areas and reference areas located on the same ecological sites. Of course, monitoring priorities and funding resources must be considered in planning and establishing monitoring studies on reference areas.

# III. STUDY DESIGN AND ANALYSIS

The rangeland monitoring methods described in Section V have a number of common elements. Those that relate to permanently marking and documenting the study location are described in detail below.

Also discussed in this section are statistical considerations (target populations, random sampling, systematic sampling, confidence intervals, etc.) and other important factors (properly identifying plant species and training people so they follow the correct procedures).

It is important to read this chapter before referring to the specific methods described in Section V, since the material covered here will not be repeated for each of them.

*Permanently Marking the Study Location*  Permanently mark the location of each study by means of a reference post (steel post) placed about 100 feet from the actual study location. Record the bearing and distance from the post to the study location. An alternative is to select a reference point, such as a prominent natural or man-made feature, and record the bearing and distance from that point to the study location. If a post is used, it should be tagged to indicate that it marks the location of a monitoring study and should not be disturbed.

Permanently mark the study location itself by driving angle iron stakes into the ground at randomly selected starting points. The baseline technique requires that both ends of the baseline be permanently staked. With the macroplot technique, a minimum of three corners need to be permanently staked. If the linear technique is used, only the beginning point of the study needs to be permanently staked. Establish the study according to the directions found in Section III.A.2 beginning on page 8.

Paint the transect location stake with brightly colored permanent spray paint (yellow or orange) to aid in relocation. Repaint this stake when subsequent readings are made.

*Study Documentation*  Document the study and transect locations, number of transects, starting points, bearings, length, distance between transects, number of quadrats, sampling interval, quadrat frame size, size of plots in a nested plot frame technique, number of cover points per quadrat frame, and other pertinent information concerning a study on the Study Location and Documentation Data form (see Appendix A). For studies that use a baseline technique, record the location of each transect along the baseline and the direction (left or right).

Be sure to document the exact location of the study site and the directions for relocating it. For example: *1.2 miles from the allotment boundary fence on the Old County Line Road. The reference post is on the south side of the road, 50 feet from the road.*

Plot the precise location of the study on detailed maps and/or aerial photos.

## A. Planning the Study

Proper planning is by far the most important part of a monitoring study. Much wasted time and effort can be avoided by proper planning. A few important considerations are discussed below. The reader should refer to Technical Reference, *Measuring & Monitoring Plant Populations*, for a more complete discussion of these important steps.

1. *Identify Objectives* Based on land use and activity plans, identify objectives appropriate for the area to be monitored. The intent is to evaluate the effects of management actions on achieving objectives by sampling specific vegetation attributes.

2. *Design the Study* The number of quadrats, points, or transects (sample size) needed depends on the objectives and the efficiency of the sampling design. It should be known before beginning the study how the data will be analyzed. The frequency of data collection (e.g., every year, every other year, etc.) and data sheet design should be determined before studies are implemented. The sample data sheets included with each method (following the narrative) are only examples of data forms. Field offices have the option to modify these forms or develop their own.

All of the methods described in this document can be established using the following techniques:

a **Baseline** A baseline is established by stretching a tape measure of any desired length between two stakes (figure 1). For an extremely long baseline, intermediate stakes can be used to ensure proper alignment. It is recommended that metric measurement be used. Individual transects are then run perpendicular to the baseline at random locations along the tape. The location of quadrats along these transects can be either measured or paced. Transects can all be run in the same direction, in which case the baseline forms one of the outer boundaries of the sampled area, or in two directions, in which case the baseline runs through the center of the sampled area. If transects are run in two directions, the direction for each individual transect should be determined randomly. (Directions for randomly selecting the location of transects to be run off of a baseline using a random numbers table are given in Appendix D). Quadrats or observation points are spaced at specified distances along the transect. This study design is intended to randomly sample a specified area. The area to be sampled can be expanded as necessary by lengthening the baseline and/or increasing the length between quadrats or sampling points.

This design may need to be modified for riparian areas or other areas where the area to be sampled is long and narrow. For these areas, a single linear transect may be more appropriate.

b **Macroplot** The concept with this type of design is to allow every area within the study site or sample area to have an equal chance to be sampled. A macroplot is a large square or rectangular study site. The size of the macroplot will depend on the size of the study site. The macroplot should encompass most of the study site. From the standpoint of statistical inference, it is best, once the macroplot boundaries have been determined, to redefine the study site to equal the macroplot. Examples of macroplot sizes are 50 m x 100 m, 100 m x 100 m, and 100 m x 200 m, but much larger macroplots can be used to cover larger study sites. Macroplot size and shape should be tailored to each situation.

## Study Layout

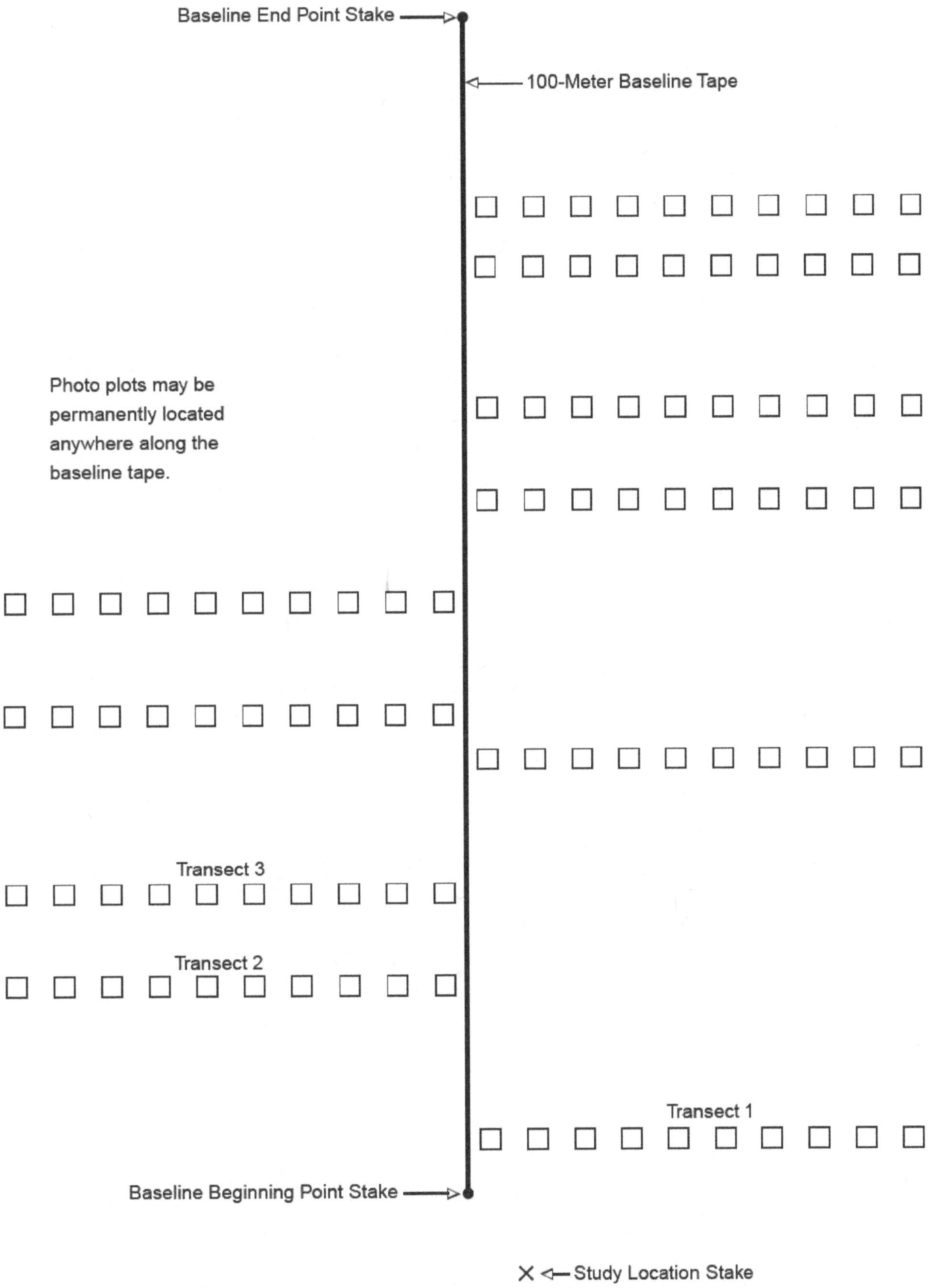

Baseline End Point Stake ⟶

100-Meter Baseline Tape

Photo plots may be permanently located anywhere along the baseline tape.

Transect 3

Transect 2

Transect 1

Baseline Beginning Point Stake ⟶

✕ ⟵ Study Location Stake

**Figure 1.** Study layout for the baseline technique.

Macroplot size also depends on the size and shape of the quadrats that will be used to sample it. The sides of the macroplot should be of dimensions that are multiples of the sides of the quadrats.

(1) *Macroplot layout* Pick one corner of the macroplot to serve as the beginning for sampling purposes. Drive an angle iron location stake into the ground at this corner. Determine the bearing of the macroplot side that will serve as the x-axis, run a tape in that direction and put an angle iron stake at the selected distance. This serves as another corner of the macroplot. Leave the x-axis tape in place for sampling purposes. Return to the origin and determine the bearing of the y-axis, which will be perpendicular to the x-axis. Run a second tape along the y-axis and put an angle iron stake in the ground at the selected distance. This serves as the third corner of the macroplot. If desired, a fourth stake may be placed at the remaining corner, but this is not necessary for sampling since sampling will be done using the two tapes serving as the x- and y-axes. See Figure 2 for an example. Leave the tapes in place until the first year's sampling is completed.

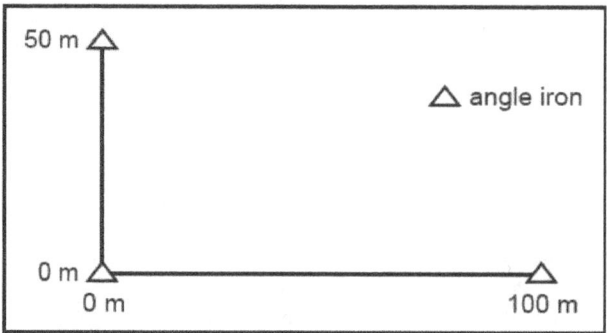

**Figure 2.** The two sides of a 50 m x 100 m macroplot, delineated by two tape measures. Both tapes begin with their 0 point at the beginning. Note placement of angle irons at three of the corners.

Be sure to document the directions of the x- and y-axes so that the macroplot can be reconstructed if one of the angle iron stakes is missing.

(2) *Quadrat locations* Quadrats are located in the macroplot using a coordinate system to identify the lower left-hand corner of each quadrat.

(a) For example it has been determined from the pilot study that 40 samples are needed using a 1 m by 16 m quadrat. The quadrats are to be positioned so that the long side is parallel to the x-axis. On a 40 m x 80 m study site (see Figure 3), the x-axis would be the 80 m side. The total number of quadrats (N) that could be placed in that 40 m x 80 m rectangle *without overlap* comprises the sampled population. In this case, N is equal to 200 quadrats.

(b) Along the x-axis there are 5 possible starting points (which always occur at the lower left-hand corner of each quadrat) for each 1 m x 16 m quadrat (at points 0 m, 16 m, 32 m, 48 m, and 64 m). Number these points 0 to 4 (in whole numbers) accordingly. Along the y-axis there are 40 possible starting points for each quadrat (at points 0 m, 1 m, 2 m, 3 m, 4 m, and so on until point 39 m). Number these points 0 to 39 accordingly (again in whole numbers)

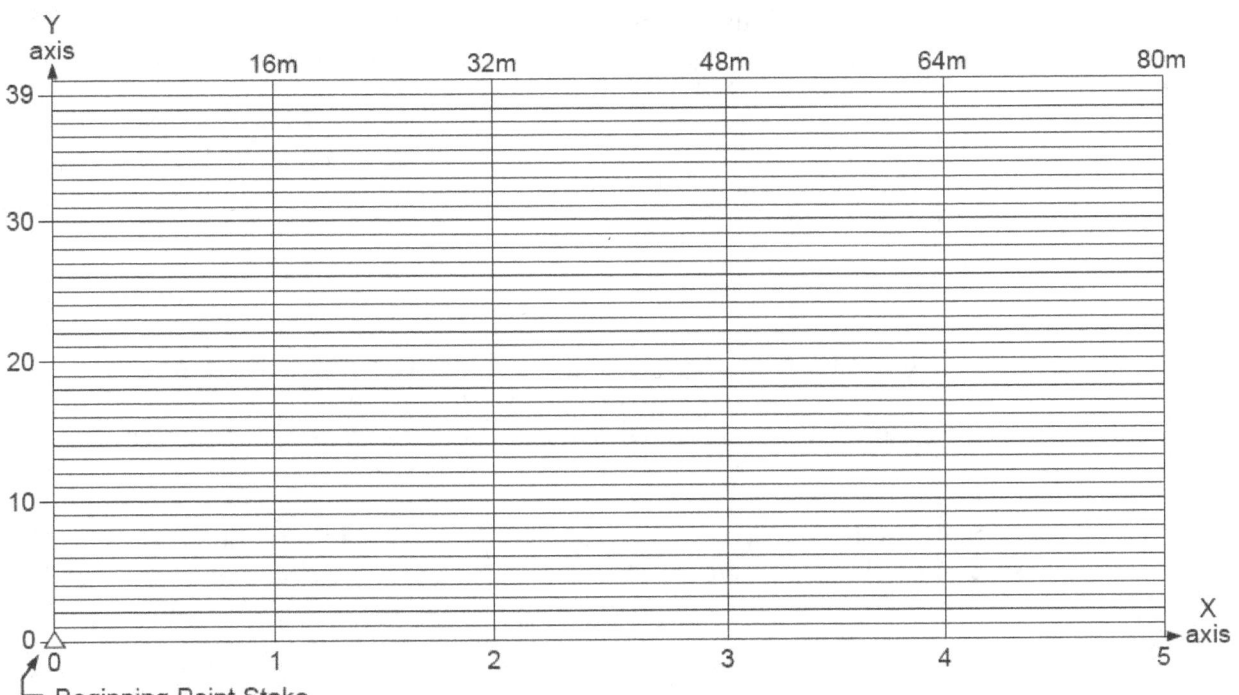

**Figure 3.** A 40 m x 80 m macroplot showing the 200 possible quadrats of size 1 m x 16 m that could be placed within it (assuming the long side of the quadrats is oriented along the x-axis).

(c) Now, using a random number table or a random number generator on a computer or handheld calculator, choose at random 40 numbers from 0 to 4 for the x axis and 40 numbers from 0 to 39 for the y axis. (Directions on the use of random number tables and random number generators are given in Appendix D of this document and in Technical Reference, *Measuring & Monitoring Plant Populations*.

(d) At the end of this process, 40 pairs of coordinates will be selected. If any pair of coordinates is repeated, the second pair is rejected and another pair picked at random to replace it (because sampling is without replacement). Continue until there are 40 unique pairs of coordinates.

These 40 pairs of coordinates mark the points at which quadrats will be positioned.

(e) Both to increase sampling efficiency and to reduce impacts to the sampling units by examiners, the coordinates should be ordered from smallest to largest first on the axis parallel to the longest side of the quadrat and then on the other axis. For example, the following four sets of coordinates have been randomly selected (presented in the order they were selected):

|  | x-axis | y-axis |
|---|---|---|
| 1. | 3 (48.0 m) | 27.0 m |
| 2. | 4 (64.0 m) | 34.0 m |
| 3. | 3 (48.0 m) | 8.0 m |
| 4. | 1 (16.0 m) | 28.0 m |

Because the quadrats are being placed with their long side parallel to the x-axis, the coordinates are ordered first by the x-axis and next by the y-axis. Thus the new order is as follows:

|    | x-axis  | y-axis  |
|----|---------|---------|
| 1. | 16.0 m  | 28.0 m  |
| 2. | 48.0 m  | 8.0 m   |
| 3. | 48.0 m  | 27.0 m  |
| 4. | 64.0 m  | 34.0 m  |

In each column defined by an x-coordinate, sampling starts from the bottom of the macroplot and moves to the top. This systematic approach ensures that quadrats are not walked on until after they have been read.

c **Linear** This study design samples a study site in a straight line. Because it samples such a small segment of the sample area, this technique is not recommended except for long, narrow study sites such as riparian areas.

Randomly select the beginning point of the transect within the study site and mark it with a stake to permanently locate the transect (figure 4). Randomly determine the transect bearing and select a prominent distant landmark such as a peak, rocky point, etc., that can be used as the transect bearing point. Vegetation attribute readings are taken at a specified interval (paced or measured) along the transect bearing. If the examiner is unable to collect an adequate sample with this transect before leaving the study site, additional transects can be run from the transect location stake at different bearings.

# B. Statistical Considerations

1. *Target Population* Study sites are selected (subjectively) that hopefully reflect what is happening on a larger area. These may be areas that are considered to be representative of a larger area such as a pasture (see Section II.D.2 for more discussion of key areas) or critical areas such as sites where endangered species occur. Monitoring studies are then located in these areas. Since these study sites are subjectively selected, no valid statistical projections to an entire allotment are possible. Therefore, careful consideration and good professional judgement must be used in selecting these sites to ensure the validity of any conclusions reached.

a Although it would be convenient to make inferences from sampling study sites regarding the larger areas they are chosen to represent, there is no way this can be done in the statistical sense because the study sites have been chosen subjectively.

b For this reason it is important to develop objectives that are specific to these study sites. It is equally important to make it clear what actions will be taken based on what happens on the study sites.

c It is also important to base objectives and management actions on each study site separately. Values from study sites from different strata should never be averaged.

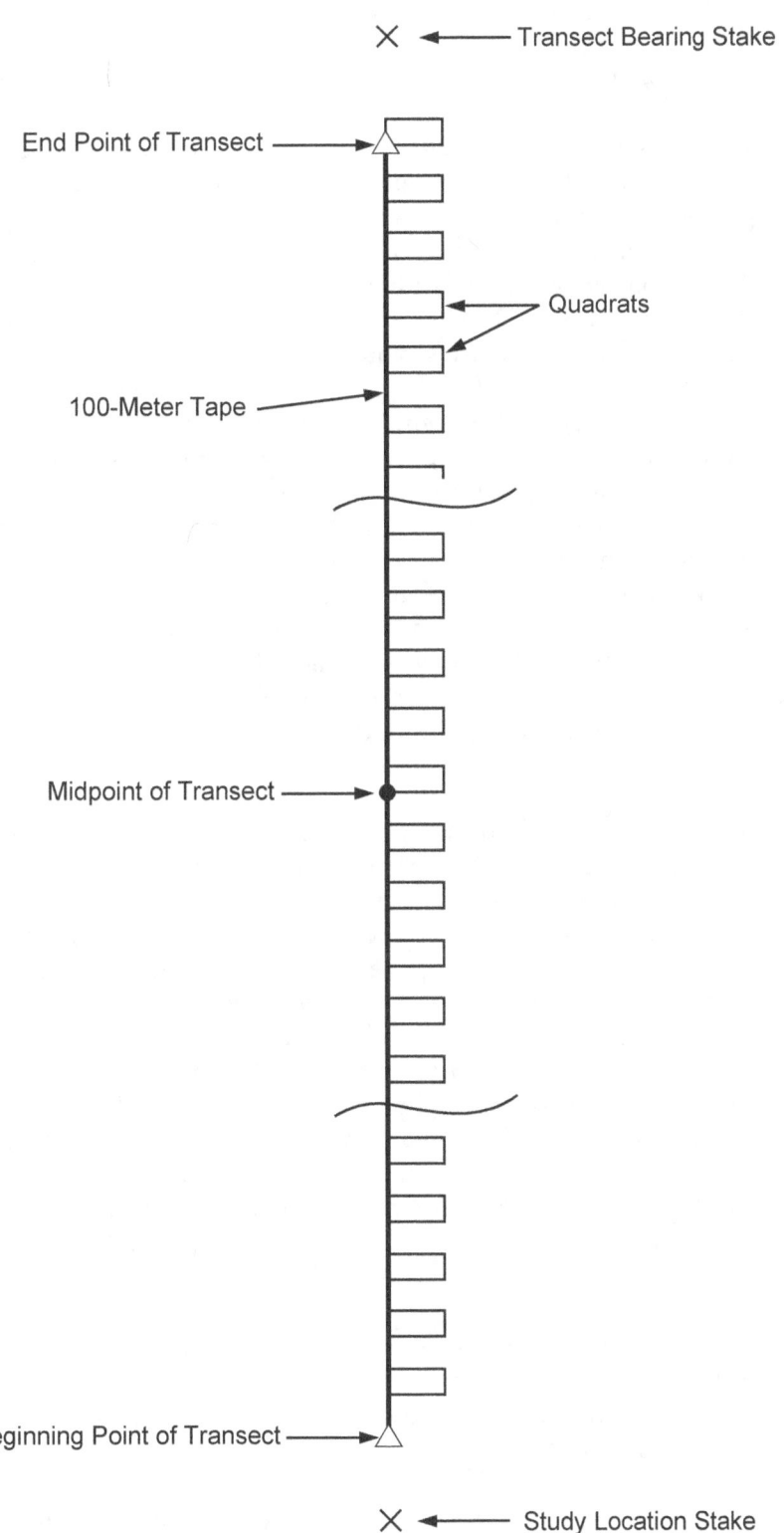

X ← Transect Bearing Stake

End Point of Transect →

Quadrats

100-Meter Tape →

Midpoint of Transect →

Beginning Point of Transect →

X ← Study Location Stake

**Figure 4.** Study layout for the linear technique.

**d** From a sampling perspective, it is the study site that constitutes the *target population*. The collection of all possible sampling units that could be placed in the study site is the target population.

2. *Random Sampling* Critical to valid monitoring study design is that the sample be drawn randomly from the population of interest. There are several methods of random sampling, many of which are discussed briefly below, but the important point is that all of the statistical analysis techniques available are based on knowing the probability of selecting a particular sampling unit. If some type of random selection of sampling units is not incorporated into the study design, the probability of selection cannot be determined and no statistical inferences can be made about the population. (Directions for randomly selecting the location of transects to be run off of a baseline using random number tables are given in Appendix D).

3. *Systematic Sampling* Systematic sampling is very common in sampling vegetation. The placement of quadrats along a transect is an example of systematic sampling. To illustrate, let's say we decide to place ten 1-square-meter quadrats at 5-meter (or 5-pace) intervals along a 50-meter transect. We randomly select a number between 0 and 4 to represent the starting point for the first quadrat along the transect and place the remaining 9 quadrats at 5-meter intervals from this starting point. Thus, if 10 observations are to be made at 5-meter intervals and the randomly selected number between 0 and 4 is 2, then the first observation is made at 2 meters and the remaining observations will be placed at 7, 12, 17, 22, 27, 32, 37, 42, and 47 meters along the transect. The selection of the starting point for systematic sampling must be random.

Strictly speaking, systematic sampling is analogous to simple random sampling only when the population being sampled is in random order (for example, see Williams 1978). Many natural populations exhibit an aggregated (also called clumped) spatial distribution pattern. This means that nearby units tend to be similar to (correlated with) each other. If, in a systematic sample, the sampling units are spaced far enough apart to reduce this correlation, the systematic sample will tend to furnish a better average and smaller standard error than is the case with a random sample, because with a completely random sample one is more likely to end up with at least some sampling units close together (see Milne 1959 and the discussion of sampling an ordered population in Scheaffer et al. 1979).

4. *Sampling vs. Nonsampling Errors* In any monitoring study, it pays to keep the error rate as low as possible. Errors can be separated into sampling errors and nonsampling errors.

   **a Sampling Errors** Sampling errors arise from chance variation; they do not result from "mistakes" such as misidentifying a species. They occur when the sample does not reflect the true population. The magnitude of sampling errors *can* be measured.

   **b Nonsampling Errors** Nonsampling errors are "mistakes" that cannot be measured.

Examples of nonsampling errors include the following:

- Using biased selection rules, such as selecting "representative samples" by subjectively locating sampling units or substituting sampling units that are "easier" to measure.

- Using sampling units in which it is impossible to accurately count or estimate the attribute in question.

- Sloppy field work.

- Transcription and recording errors.

- Incorrect or inconsistent species identification.

To minimize nonsampling errors:

- Design studies to minimize nonsampling errors. For example, if canopy cover estimates are needed, point intercept or line intercept techniques result in smaller nonsampling errors than the use of quadrats (Floyd and Anderson 1987; Kennedy and Addison 1987; Buckner 1985). For density data, select a quadrat size that doesn't contain too many individual plants, stems, etc., to count accurately.

- When different personnel are used, conduct rigorous training and testing to ensure consistency in measurement and estimation.

- Design field forms that are easy to use and not confusing to data transcribers. Double (or triple) check all data entered into computer programs to ensure the numbers are correct.

5. *Confidence Interval* In rangeland monitoring, the true population total (or any other true population parameter) will never be known. The best way to judge how well a sample estimates the true population total is by calculating a *confidence interval*. The confidence interval is a range of values that is expected to include the true population size (or any other parameter of interest, often an average) a given percentage of the time (Krebs 1989). For instructions in calculating confidence intervals, see Technical Reference, *Measuring & Monitoring Plant Populations*.

6. *Quadrat Size and Shape* Quadrat size and shape can have a major influence on the precision of the estimate.

   a **Frequency** Frequency is most typically measured in square quadrats. Because only presence or absence is measured, square quadrats are fine for this purpose. Of most concern in frequency measurement is the size of the quadrat. Good sensitivity to change is obtained for frequency values between 20 percent and 80 percent (Despain et al. 1991). Frequency values between 10 percent and 90 percent are still useful, but values outside this range should be used only to indicate species presence, not to detect change (Despain et al. 1991). Because frequency values are measured separately for each species, what constitutes an optimum size quadrat for one species may be less than optimum or even inappropriate for another. This problem is partially resolved by using nested plot quadrats of different sizes (refer to Frequency Method, Section V.B).

b **Cover** In general, quadrats are not recommended for estimating cover (Floyd and Anderson 1987; Kennedy and Addison 1987). Where they are used, the same types of considerations given below for density apply: long, thin quadrats will likely be better than circular, square, or shorter and wider rectangular quadrats (Krebs 1989). Each situation, however, should be analyzed separately. The amount of area in the quadrat is a concern with cover estimation. The larger the area, the more difficult it is to accurately estimate cover.

c **Density** Long, thin quadrats are better (often very much better) than circles, squares, or shorter and wider quadrats. How narrow the quadrats can be depends upon consideration of problems of edge effect, although problems of edge effect can be largely eliminated by developing consistent rules for determining whether to include or exclude plants that fall directly under quadrat edges. One recommendation is to count plants that are rooted directly under the top and left sides of the quadrat but not those directly rooted under the bottom and right quadrat sides. The amount of area within the quadrat is limited by the degree of accuracy with which one can count all the plants within each quadrat.

d **Plant Biomass** For the same reason as given for density, long, thin quadrats are likely to be better than circular, square, or shorter and wider rectangular quadrats (Krebs 1989). Edge effect can result in significant measurement bias if the quadrats are too small (Wiegert 1962). Since above-ground vegetation must be clipped in some quadrats, circular quadrats should be avoided because of the difficulty in cutting around the perimeter of the circle with hand shears and the likely measurement bias that would result. If plant biomass is collected in grams, it can be easily converted to pounds per acres if the total area sampled is a multiple of 9.6 ft².

Use the following table to convert grams to pounds per acre:

**Table 1**

| (# of plots x size | | = total area) | | | | |
|---|---|---|---|---|---|---|
| (10 x 0.96 | = | 9.6 ft²) | multiply grams times | 100 | = | pounds per acre |
| (10 x 1.92 | = | 19.2 ft²) | multiply grams times | 50 | = | pounds per acre |
| (10 x 2.40 | = | 24.0 ft²) | multiply grams times | 40 | = | pounds per acre |
| (10 x 4.80 | = | 48.0 ft²) | multiply grams times | 20 | = | pounds per acre |
| (10 x 9.60 | = | 96.0 ft²) | multiply grams times | 10 | = | pounds per acre |
| (10 x 96.0 | = | 960.0 ft²) | multiply grams times | 1 | = | pounds per acre |

7. *Interspersion* One of the most important considerations of sampling is good interspersion of sampling units throughout the area to be sampled (the target population).

The basic goal should be to have sampling units as well interspersed as possible throughout the area of the target population. The practice of placing all of the sampling units, whether they be quadrats or points, along a single transect or even a few transects should be avoided, because it results in poor interspersion of sampling units and makes it unlikely that the sample will provide a representative sample of the target population. This is true even if the transect(s) is randomly located.

8. *Pilot Studies* The purposes of pilot studies are to select the optimum size and/

or shape of the sampling unit for the study and to determine how much variability exists in the population being sampled. The latter information is necessary to determine the sample size necessary to meet specific management and monitoring objectives.

**a** **Initial Considerations** Before beginning the actual pilot study, subjectively experiment with different sizes and shapes of sampling units. For example, if estimating density, subjectively place quadrats[1] of a certain size and shape in areas with large numbers of the target plant species. Then see how many plants fall into the quadrat and ascertain if this is too many to count. See what kind of problems there might be with edge effect: when individuals fall on or near one of the long edges of the quadrat, will it be difficult for examiners to make consistent calls as to whether these individuals are in or out of the quadrat?[2] See if there is a tendency to get more plants in rectangular quadrats when they are run one way as opposed to another. If so, then the quadrats should be run in the direction that hits the most plants. Otherwise it is likely that some quadrats will have few to no plants in them, while others will have many; this is highly undesirable. The goal should be to end up with similar numbers of plants in each of the quadrats, while still sampling at random.

If transects or lines are the sampling units, subjectively lay out lines of different lengths and in different directions. See if the lines cross most of the variability likely to be encountered with respect to the target plant species. If not, they may need to be longer. Don't make the lines so long, however, that it will be difficult to measure them, especially if there are a lot of lines involved. As with rectangular quadrats, it is desirable to have each of the lines encountering similar numbers and/or cover values of the target species, while still sampling at random.

**b** **Efficiency of Sample Design** Pilot sampling allows the examiner to compare the efficiency of various sampling designs. By dividing the sample standard deviation by the sample average, the coefficient of variation is obtained. Comparing coefficients of variation allows one to determine which of two or more sampling designs is most efficient (the lower the coefficient of variation, the greater the efficiency of the sampling design).

Conduct a pilot study by randomly positioning a number of sampling units of different sizes and shapes within the area to be sampled and then choosing the size and shape that yields the smallest coefficient of variation.

The following shows how to calculate the standard deviation for the density of

---

[1] Note that it is not necessary to construct an actual frame for the quadrats used. It is sufficient to delineate quadrats using a combination of tape measures and meter (or yard) sticks. For example, a 5 m x 0.25 m quadrat can be constructed by selecting a 5 m interval along a meter tape, placing two 1-meter sticks perpendicular to the tape at both ends of the interval (with their zero points at the tape), and laying another tape or rope across these sticks at their 0.25 m points. This then circumscribes a quadrat of the desired size and shape.

[2] Often, problems with edge effect can be largely overcome by making a rule that any plants that fall on the left or top edges of the quadrat *are* counted, whereas any plants that fall on the right or bottom edges of the quadrat *are not* counted.

sideoats grama occurring in two sample designs. In this example there are 2, 10, and 21 sideoats grama plants in three separate quadrats in the first design and 9, 10, and 14 sideoats grama plants in the second set of three plots. The average number of plants in both sets of plots is 11 (2+10+21= 33/3= 11 and 9+10+14= 33/3=11). The standard deviation is calculated as follows:

$$S = \sqrt{\frac{(X_1 - \overline{X})^2 + (X_2 - \overline{X})^2 + \ldots + (X_n - \overline{X})^2}{n-1}} \quad or \quad S = \sqrt{\frac{\sum (X - \overline{X})^2}{n-1}}$$

where:
$S$ = standard deviation
$X$ = number of plants
$\overline{X}$ = the mean or average number of plants per quadrat
$n$ = the number of samples (quadrats in this example)

| Number of plants | Deviation $(X - \overline{X})$ | Squared Deviation $(X - \overline{X})^2$ |
|---|---|---|
| 2 | 2 - 11 = -9 | 81 |
| 10 | 10 - 11 = -1 | 1 |
| 21 | 21 - 11 = 10 | 100 |
| $\overline{X}$ = 33/3 = 11 | | 182 |

$$S = \sqrt{\frac{\sum (X - \overline{X})^2}{n-1}} = \sqrt{\frac{182}{3-1}} = \sqrt{\frac{182}{2}} = \sqrt{91} = 9.54$$

| Number of plants | Deviation $(X - \overline{X})$ | Squared Deviation $(X - \overline{X})^2$ |
|---|---|---|
| 9 | 9 - 11 = -2 | 4 |
| 10 | 10 - 11 = -1 | 1 |
| 14 | 14 - 11 = 3 | 9 |
| $\overline{X}$ = 33/3 = 11 | | 14 |

$$S = \sqrt{\frac{\sum (X - \overline{X})^2}{n-1}} = \sqrt{\frac{14}{3-1}} = \sqrt{\frac{14}{2}} = \sqrt{7} = 2.65$$

The coefficient of variation for the first set of quadrats is 9.54/11 or .86, whereas the second set of quadrats has a coefficient of variation of 2.65/11= .24. Since the second sampling design has the lowest coefficient of variation, it is the most efficient design.

*This example, with only three quadrats in each sampling design, is given solely to show how to calculate standard deviations and coefficients of variation. When comparing actual study designs, ensure that the sample standard deviation is a good estimate of the population standard deviation. One way of ensuring this is to construct sequential sampling graphs of the standard deviation of each design (see Sequential Sampling below).*

Wiegert (1962), summarized in Krebs (1989:67-72), gives a quantitative method for determining optimal quadrat size and/or shape. The method considers the costs involved in locating and measuring quadrats and the standard deviation (or its square, the variance) that results from samples of that size and shape. Refer to Krebs' book for details (and an example).

c **Sequential Sampling** The estimate of the standard deviation derived through pilot sampling is one of the values used to calculate sample size, whether one uses the formulas given in Technical Reference, *Measuring & Monitoring Plant Populations*, or uses a computer program.

When conducting the pilot sampling, employ sequential sampling. Sequential sampling helps determine whether the examiner has taken a large enough pilot sample to properly evaluate different sampling designs and/or to use the standard deviation from the pilot sample to calculate sample size. The process is accomplished as follows:

Gather pilot sampling data using some arbitrarily selected sample size. Calculate the average and standard deviation for the first two quadrats, calculate it again after putting in the next quadrat value, and continue these iterative calculations after the addition of each quadrat value to the sample. This will generate a running average and standard deviation. Look at the four columns of numbers on the right of Figure 5 for an example of how to carry out this procedure.

Plot on graph paper (or use a computer program) the sample size versus the average and standard deviation. Look for curves smoothing out. In the example shown in Figure 5, the curves smooth out after n = 30-35. The decision to stop sampling is a subjective one. There are no hard and fast rules.

A computer is valuable for creating sequential sampling graphs. Spreadsheet programs such as Lotus 1-2-3 allow for entering the data in a form that can later be analyzed while at the same time creating a sequential sampling graph of the running average and standard deviation. This further allows the examiner to look at several random sequences of the data before deciding on the number of sampling units to measure.

Use the sequential sampling method to determine what sample size not to use (don't use a sample size below the point where the running average and standard deviation have not stabilized). Plug the final average and standard deviation information into the appropriate sample size equation to actually determine the necessary sample size.

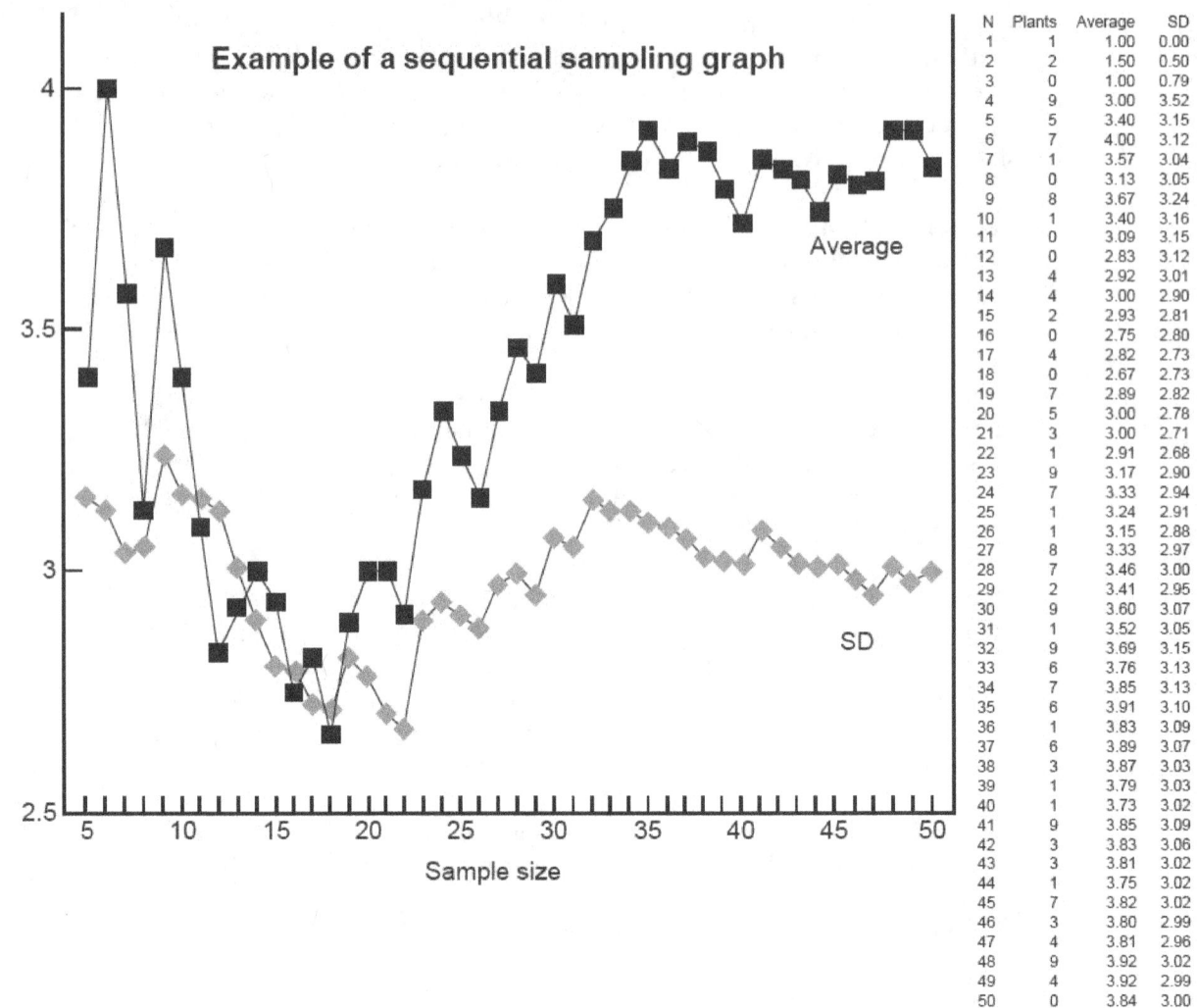

| N | Plants | Average | SD |
|---|---|---|---|
| 1 | 1 | 1.00 | 0.00 |
| 2 | 2 | 1.50 | 0.50 |
| 3 | 0 | 1.00 | 0.79 |
| 4 | 9 | 3.00 | 3.52 |
| 5 | 5 | 3.40 | 3.15 |
| 6 | 7 | 4.00 | 3.12 |
| 7 | 1 | 3.57 | 3.04 |
| 8 | 0 | 3.13 | 3.05 |
| 9 | 8 | 3.67 | 3.24 |
| 10 | 1 | 3.40 | 3.16 |
| 11 | 0 | 3.09 | 3.15 |
| 12 | 0 | 2.83 | 3.12 |
| 13 | 4 | 2.92 | 3.01 |
| 14 | 4 | 3.00 | 2.90 |
| 15 | 2 | 2.93 | 2.81 |
| 16 | 0 | 2.75 | 2.80 |
| 17 | 4 | 2.82 | 2.73 |
| 18 | 0 | 2.67 | 2.73 |
| 19 | 7 | 2.89 | 2.82 |
| 20 | 5 | 3.00 | 2.78 |
| 21 | 3 | 3.00 | 2.71 |
| 22 | 1 | 2.91 | 2.68 |
| 23 | 9 | 3.17 | 2.90 |
| 24 | 7 | 3.33 | 2.94 |
| 25 | 1 | 3.24 | 2.91 |
| 26 | 1 | 3.15 | 2.88 |
| 27 | 8 | 3.33 | 2.97 |
| 28 | 7 | 3.46 | 3.00 |
| 29 | 2 | 3.41 | 2.95 |
| 30 | 9 | 3.60 | 3.07 |
| 31 | 1 | 3.52 | 3.05 |
| 32 | 9 | 3.69 | 3.15 |
| 33 | 6 | 3.76 | 3.13 |
| 34 | 7 | 3.85 | 3.13 |
| 35 | 6 | 3.91 | 3.10 |
| 36 | 1 | 3.83 | 3.09 |
| 37 | 6 | 3.89 | 3.07 |
| 38 | 3 | 3.87 | 3.03 |
| 39 | 1 | 3.79 | 3.03 |
| 40 | 1 | 3.73 | 3.02 |
| 41 | 9 | 3.85 | 3.09 |
| 42 | 3 | 3.83 | 3.06 |
| 43 | 3 | 3.81 | 3.02 |
| 44 | 1 | 3.75 | 3.02 |
| 45 | 7 | 3.82 | 3.02 |
| 46 | 3 | 3.80 | 2.99 |
| 47 | 4 | 3.81 | 2.96 |
| 48 | 9 | 3.92 | 3.02 |
| 49 | 4 | 3.92 | 2.99 |
| 50 | 0 | 3.84 | 3.00 |

**Figure 5.** Example of a sequential sampling graph. The running average and standard deviation are plotted for sample sizes of n=5 up to n=50. Sampling was conducted in an area of 50 m x 100 m with a quadrat size of 1 m x 5 m. Actual values are shown on the right.

9. *Sample size determination* An adequate sample is vital to the success of any monitoring effort. Adequacy relates to the ability of the observer to evaluate whether the management objective has been achieved. It makes little sense, for example, to set a management objective of increasing the density of a rare plant species by 20 percent when the monitoring design and sample size is unlikely to detect changes in density of less than 50 percent. The question of sample size determination is addressed in much more detail in Technical Reference, *Measuring & Monitoring Plant Populations*.

Formulas for calculating sample sizes are given in the Technical Reference, *Planning for Monitoring*. Because these formulas are rather unwieldy, you may choose to use a computer program. There are several microcomputer programs that will calculate sample size, most of which are available for reasonable cost. Examples are the programs DESIGN (by SYSTAT), EXSAMPLE, *N*, Nsurv, PASS, and SOLO Power Analysis. Goldstein (1989) reviews 13 different computer programs that can calculate sample sizes. STPLAN Version 4.0, a DOS-based program developed by Brown et al. (1993), is available as freeware from the following Internet ftp (file transfer protocol) site: odin.mda.uth.tmc.edu. Documentation is included with the program. The program calculates sample sizes needed for all of the types of significance testing but does not calculate those required for estimating a single population average, total, or proportion. PC-SIZE: CONSULTANT is a shareware program that will calculate sample sizes for estimating an average (but not a proportion) and for all the types of significance tests. It was developed in 1990 by Gerard E. Dallal, who also developed the commercial program DESIGN discussed above. PC-SIZE: CONSULTANT appears to contain all of the algorithms included in DESIGN but at a fraction of the cost (the author asks for a fee of $15.00 if the user finds the program to be useful). The program is available via the World Wide Web at the following address:

http://www.coast.net/SimTel/SimTel/

Once at the homepage, change to the directory msdos/statstic/ and download the file st-size.zip. Unzip the file using the shareware program PKUNZIP. Executable files and documentation are included.

Alternatively, tables can be used to calculate sample size. For detecting change in averages, proportions, or totals between two time periods, the tables found in Cohen (1988) are highly recommended.

10. *Graphical Display of Data* The use of graphs, both to initially explore the quality of the monitoring data collected and to display the results of the data analysis, is important to designing and implementing monitoring studies. See Technical Reference, *Measuring & Monitoring Plant Populations*, for descriptions of these graphs, along with examples.

a **Graphs to Examine Study Data Prior to Analysis** The best of these graphs plot each data point. These graphs can help determine whether the data meet the assumptions of parametric statistics, or whether the data set contains outliers (data with values much lower or much higher than most of the rest of the data—as might occur if one made a mistake in measuring or recording). Normal probability plots and box plots are two of the most useful types for this purpose. Graphs can also assist in determining appropriate quadrat size. For more information, see Technical Reference, *Measuring & Monitoring Plant Populations*.

b **Graphs to Display the Results of Data Analysis** Rather than displaying each data point, these graphs display summary statistics (i.e., averages, totals, or proportions). When these summary statistics are graphed, error bars must be used to display the precision of estimates. Because it is the true parameter (average, median, total, or proportion) that is of interest, confidence intervals should be used as error bars. Types of graphs include:

- Bar charts with confidence intervals.

- Graphs of summary statistics plotted as points, with error bars.

- Box plots with "notches" for error bars.

## C. Other Important Considerations

1. *Sampling All Species* Although the key species concept is important in analyzing and evaluating management actions, other species should also be considered for sampling. Whenever possible, all species should be sampled, especially on the initial sampling. It is also important to record sampling data by individual species rather than by genera, form class, or other grouping. These data can be lumped later during the analysis if appropriate. Both of these approaches will provide greater flexibility in data analysis if objectives or key species change in the future.

2. *Plant Species Identification* The plant species must be properly identified in order for the data to be useful in grazing allotment, wildlife habitat area, herd management area, watershed area, or other designated management area evaluations. In some cases, it may be helpful to include pressed plant specimens, photographs, or other aids used for species identification in the study file. If data are collected prior to positive species identification, examiners should collect plant specimens for later verification.

3. *Training* The purpose of training is to provide resource specialists with the necessary skills for implementing studies and collecting reliable, unbiased, and consistent data. Examiners should understand data collection, documentation, analysis, interpretation, and evaluation procedures, including the need for uniformity, accuracy, and reliable monitoring data.

   Training should occur in the field by qualified personnel to ensure that examiners are familiar with the equipment and supplies and that detailed procedural instructions are thoroughly demonstrated and understood.

   As a follow-up to the training, data collected should be examined early in the study effort to ensure that the data are properly collected and recorded.

   Periodic review and/or recalibration during the field season may be necessary for maintaining consistency among examiners because of progressive phenological changes. Review and recalibration during each field season are especially important where data collection methods require estimates rather than direct measurements.

# IV. ATTRIBUTES

The following is a matrix of monitoring techniques and vegetation attributes that are described in this reference. The X indicates that this is the primary attribute that the technique collects. Some techniques have the capability of collecting other attributes; the • indicates the secondary attribute that can be collected or calculated.

| Method | Frequency | Cover | Density | Production | Structure | Composition |
|---|---|---|---|---|---|---|
| Frequency | X | • | | | | |
| Dry-weight-Rank | • | | | • | | X[3] |
| Daubenmire | • | X | | | | • |
| Line Intercept | | X | | | | • |
| Step Point | | X | | | | • |
| Point Intercept | | X | | | | • |
| Density | | | X | | | • |
| Double Weight Sampling | | | | X | | • |
| Harvest | | | | X | | • |
| Comparative Yield | | | | X | | • |
| Cover Board | | X | | | X | |
| Robel Pole | | | | • | X | |

## A. Frequency

*1. Description* Frequency is one of the easiest and fastest methods available for monitoring vegetation. It describes the abundance and distribution of species and is useful to detect changes in a plant community over time.

Frequency has been used to determine rangeland condition but only limited work has been done in most communities. This makes the interpretation difficult. The literature has discussed the relationship between density and frequency but this relationship is only consistent with randomly distributed plants (Greig-Smith 1983).

---

[3] Species composition is calculated using production data. Frequency data should not be used to calculate species composition.

Frequency is the number of times a species is present in a given number of sampling units. It is usually expressed as a percentage.

## 2. Advantages and Limitations

**a** Frequency is highly influenced by the size and shape of the quadrats used. Quadrats or nested quadrats are the most common measurement used; however, point sampling and step point methods have also been used to estimate frequency. The size and shape of a quadrat needed to adequately determine frequency depends on the distribution, number, and size of the plant species.

**b** To determine change, the frequency of a species must generally be at least 20% and no greater than 80%. Frequency comparisons must be made with quadrats of the same size and shape. While change can be detected with frequency, the extent to which the vegetation community has changed cannot be determined.

**c** High repeatability is obtainable.

**d** Frequency is highly sensitive to changes resulting from seedling establishment. Seedlings present one year may not be persistent the following year. This situation is problematic if data is collected only every few years. It is less of a problem if seedlings are recorded separately.

**e** Frequency is also very sensitive to changes in pattern of distribution in the sampled area.

**f** Rooted frequency data is less sensitive to fluctuations in climatic and biotic influences.

**g** Interpretation of changes in frequency is difficult because of the inability to determine the vegetation attribute that changed. Frequency cannot tell which of three parameters has changed: canopy cover, density, or pattern of distribution.

## 3. Appropriate Use of Frequency for Rangeland Monitoring
If the primary reason for collecting frequency data is to demonstrate that a change in vegetation has occurred, then on most sites the frequency method is capable of accomplishing the task with statistical evidence more rapidly and at less cost than any other method that is currently available (Hironaka 1985).

Frequency should not be the only data collected if time and money are available. Additional information on ground cover, plant cover, and other vegetation and site data would contribute to a better understanding of the changes that have occurred (Hironaka 1985).

West (1985) noted the following limitations: "Because of the greater risk of misjudging a downward than upward trend, frequency may provide the easiest early warning of undesirable changes in key or indicator species. However, because frequency data are so dependent on quadrat size and sensitive to non-random dispersion patterns that prevail on rangelands, managers are fooling themselves if they calculate percentage composition from frequency data and try to compare different sites at the same time or the same site over time in terms of total species composition. This is because the numbers derived for frequency sampling are unique to the choice of sample size, shape, number, and placement. For variables of cover and weight, accuracy is mostly what is affected by these choices and the variable can be conceived independently of the sampling protocol."

## B. Cover

*1. Description* Cover is an important vegetation and hydrologic characteristic. It can be used in various ways to determine the contribution of each species to a plant community. Cover is also important in determining the proper hydrologic function of a site. This characteristic is very sensitive to biotic and edaphic forces. For watershed stability, some have tried to use a standard soil cover, but research has shown each edaphic site has its own potential cover.

Cover is generally referred to as the percentage of ground surface covered by vegetation. However, numerous definitions exist. It can be expressed in absolute terms (square meters/hectares) but is most often expressed as a percentage. The objective being measured will determine the definition and type of cover measured.

a Vegetation cover is the total cover of vegetation on a site.

b Foliar cover is the area of ground covered by the vertical projection of the aerial portions of the plants. Small openings in the canopy and intraspecific overlap are excluded (Figure 6).

c Canopy cover is the area of ground covered by the vertical projection of the outermost perimeter of the natural spread of foliage of plants. Small openings within the canopy are included. It may exceed 100% (Figure 7).

**Figure 6.** Foliar cover.

**Figure 7.** Canopy cover.

d Basal cover is the area of ground surface occupied by the basal portion of the plants.

e Ground cover is the cover of plants, litter, rocks, and gravel on a site.

## 2. *Advantages and Limitations*

**a** Ground cover is most often used to determine the watershed stability of the site, but comparisons between sites are difficult to interpret because of the different potentials associated with each ecological site.

**b** Vegetation cover is a component of ground cover and is often sensitive to climatic fluctuations that can cause errors in interpretation. Canopy cover and foliar cover are components of vegetation cover and are the most sensitive to climatic and biotic factors. This is particularly true with herbaceous vegetation.

**c** Overlapping canopy cover often creates problems, particularly in mixed communities. If species composition is to be determined, the canopy of each species is counted regardless of any overlap with other species. If watershed characteristics are the objective, only the uppermost canopy is generally counted.

**d** For trend comparisons in herbaceous plant communities, basal cover is generally considered to be the most stable. It does not vary as much due to climatic fluctuations or current-year grazing.

# C. Density

## 1. *Description*
Density has been used to describe characteristics of plant communities. However, comparisons can only be based on similar life-form and size. This is why density is rarely used as a measurement by itself when describing plant communities. For example, the importance of a particular species to a community is very different if there are 1,000 annual plants per acre versus 1,000 shrubs per acre. It should be pointed out that density was synonymous with cover in the earlier literature.

Density is basically the number of individuals per unit area. The term refers to the closeness of individual plants to one another.

## 2. *Advantages and Limitations*

**a** Density is useful in monitoring threatened and endangered species or other special status plants because it samples the number of individuals per unit area.

**b** Density is useful when comparing similar life-forms (annuals to annuals, shrubs to shrubs) that are approximately the same size. For trend measurements, this parameter is used to determine if the number of individuals of a specific species is increasing or decreasing.

**c** The problem with using density is being able to identify individuals and comparing individuals of different sizes. It is often hard to identify individuals of plants that are capable of vegetative reproduction (e.g., rhizomatous plants like western wheatgrass or Gambles oak). Comparisons of bunchgrass plants to rhizomatous plants are often meaningless because of these problems. Similar problems occur when looking at the density of shrubs of different growth forms or comparing seedlings to mature plants. Density on rhizomatous or stoloniferous plants is determined by counting the number of stems instead of the number of individuals. Seedling density is directly related to environmental conditions and can often be interpreted erroneously as a positive or negative trend measurement. Because of these limitations, density has generally been used with shrubs and not herbaceous vegetation. Seedlings and mature plants should be recorded separately.

If the individuals can be identified, density measurements are repeatable over time because there is small observer error. The type of vegetation and distribution will dictate the technique used to obtain the density measurements. In homogenous plant communities, which are rare, square quadrats have been recommended, while heterogenous communities should be sampled with rectangular or line strip quadrats. Plotless methods have also been developed for widely dispersed plants.

# D. Production

### 1. *Description*  Many believe that the relative production of different species in a plant community is the best measure of these species' roles in the ecosystem.

The terminology associated with vegetation biomass is normally related to production.

**a** Gross primary production is the total amount of organic material produced, both above ground and below ground.

**b** Biomass is the total weight of living organisms in the ecosystem, including plants and animals.

**c** Standing crop is the amount of plant biomass present above ground at any given point.

**d** Peak standing crop is the greatest amount of plant biomass above ground present during a given year.

**e** Total forage is the total herbaceous and woody palatable plant biomass available to herbivores.

**f** Allocated forage is the difference of desired amount of residual material subtracted from the total forage.

**g** Browse is the portion of woody plant biomass accessible to herbivores.

### 2. *Advantages and Limitations*

**a** Biomass and gross primary production are rarely used in rangeland trend studies because it is impractical to obtain the measurements below ground. In addition, the animal portion of biomass is rarely obtainable.

**b** Standing crop and peak standing crop are the measurements most often used in trend studies. Peak standing crop is generally measured at the end of the growing season. However, different species reach their peak standing crop at different times. This can be a significant problem in mixed plant communities.

**c** Often, the greater the diversity of plant species or growth patterns, the larger the error if only one measurement is made.

**d** Other problems associated with the use of plant biomass are that fluctuations in climate and biotic influences can alter the estimates. When dealing with large ungulates, exclosures are generally required to measure this parameter. Several authors have suggested that approximately 25% of the peak standing crop is consumed by insects or trampled; this is rarely discussed in most trend studies.

**e** Collecting production data also tends to be time and labor intensive. Cover and frequency have been used to estimate plant biomass in some species.

## E. Structure

*1. Description* Structure of vegetation primarily looks at how the vegetation is arranged in a three-dimensional space. The primary use for structure measurements is to help evaluate a vegetation community's value in providing habitat for associated wildlife species.

Vegetation is measured in layers on vertical planes. Measurements generally look at the vertical distribution by either estimating the cover of each layer or by measuring the height of the vegetation.

*2. Advantages and Limitations* Structure data provide information that is useful in describing the suitability of the sites for screening and escape cover, which are important for wildlife. Methods used to collect these data are quick, allowing for numerous samples to be obtained over relatively large areas. Methods that use visual obstruction techniques to evaluate vegetation height have little observer bias. Those techniques that estimate cover require more training to reduce observer bias. Structure is rarely used by itself when describing trend.

## F. Composition

*1. Description* Composition is a calculated attribute rather than one that is directly collected in the field. It is the proportion of various plant species in relation to the total of a given area. It may be expressed in terms of relative cover, relative density, relative weight, etc.

Composition has been used extensively to describe ecological sites and to evaluate rangeland condition.

To calculate composition, the individual value (weight, density, percent cover) for a species or group of species is divided by the total value of the entire population.

## 2. *Advantages and Limitations*

a Quadrats, point sampling, and step point methods can all be used to calculate composition.

b The repeatability of determining composition depends on the attribute collected and the method used.

c Sensitivity to change is dependent on the attribute used to calculate composition. For instance, if plant biomass is used to calculate composition, the values can vary with climatic conditions and the timing of climatic events (precipitation, frost-free period, etc.). Composition based on basal cover, on the other hand, would be relatively stable.

d Composition allows the comparison of vegetation communities at various locations within the same ecological sites.

# V. METHODS

## A. Photographs

1. *General Description* Photographs and videotapes can be valuable sources of information in portraying resource values and conditions. Therefore pictures should be taken of all study areas. Both photographs and videos can be taken at photo plots or photo points. The difference between photo plots and photo points is that, with photo points, closeup photographs of a permanently marked plot on the ground are not taken. Use close-up and/or general view pictures with all of the study methods. Comparing pictures of the same site taken over a period of years furnishes visual evidence of vegetation and soil changes. In some situations, photo points could be the primary monitoring tool. All pictures should be in color, regardless of whether they are the primary or secondary monitoring tool.

2. *Equipment* The following equipment is suggested for the establishment of photo plots:

   - Study Location and Documentation Data form (see Appendix A)
   - Photo Identification Label (see Appendix C)
   - Frame to delineate the 3- x 3-foot, 5- x 5-foot, or 1- x 1- meter photo plots (see Illustrations 1 and 2)
   - Four rods to divide the 3- x 3- foot and 1- x 1-meter photo plot into nine square segments
   - Stakes of 3/4 - or 1- inch angle iron not less than 16 inches long
   - Hammer
   - 35-mm camera with a 28-mm wide-angle lens and film
   - Small step ladder (for 5- x 5-foot photo plots)
   - Felt tip pen with waterproof ink

3. *Study Identification* Number studies for proper identification to ensure that the data collected can be positively associated with specific studies on the ground (see Appendix B).

4. *Close-up Pictures* Close-up pictures show the soil surface characteristics and the amount of ground surface covered by vegetation and litter. Close-up pictures are generally taken of permanently located photo plots.

   a The location of photo plots is determined at the time the studies are established. Document the location of photo plots on the Study Location and Documentation Data form to expedite relocation (see Appendix A).

   b Generally a 3- X 3-foot square frame is used for photo plots; however, a different size and shape frame may be used. Where new studies are being established, a 1-meter x 1-meter photo plot is recommended. Frames can be made of PVC pipe, steel rods, or any similar material. Illustration 1 shows a diagram of a typical photo plot frame constructed of steel rod.

**c** Angle iron stakes are driven into the ground at two diagonal corners of the frame to permanently mark a photo plot (see Illustration 3). Paint the stakes with bright-colored permanent spray paint (yellow or orange) to aid in relocation. Repaint these stakes when subsequent pictures are taken.

**d** The Photo Identification Label is placed flat on the ground immediately adjacent to the photo plot frame (see Appendix C).

**e** The camera point, or the location from which the close-up picture is taken, should be on the north side of the photo plot so that repeat pictures can be taken at any time during the day without casting a shadow across the plot.

**f** To take the close-up pictures, stand over the photo plot with toes touching the edge of the frame. Include the photo label in the photograph. Use a 35-mm camera with a 28-mm wide-angle lens.

**g** A step ladder is needed to take close-up pictures of photo plots larger than 3- x 3-foot.

5. *General View Pictures* General view pictures present a broad view of a study site. These pictures are often helpful in relocating study sites.

**a** If a linear design is used, general view pictures may be taken from either or both ends of the transect. The points from which these pictures are taken are determined at the time the studies are established. Document the location of these points on the Study Location and Documentation Data form to expedite relocation (see Appendix A).

**b** The Photo Identification Label is placed in an upright position so that it will appear in the foreground of the photograph (see Appendix C).

**c** To take general view pictures, stand at the selected points and include the photo label, a general view of the site, and some sky in the pictures.

**d** A picture of a study site taken from the nearest road at the time of establishment of the study facilitates relocation.

6. *Photo Points* General view photographs taken from a permanent reference point are often adequate to visually portray dominant landscape vegetation. It is important that the photo point location be documented in writing and that the photo include a reference point in the foreground (fencepost, fence line, etc.), along with a distinct landmark on the skyline. Photographs taken from photo points should be brought to the field to assist in finding the photo point and to ensure that the same photograph (bearing, amount of skyline, etc.) is retaken. The photograph should be taken at roughly the same time each year to assist in interpreting changes in vegetation. As always, recording field notes to supplement the photographs is a good idea.

Photo points are especially well adapted for use by external groups who are interested in monitoring selected management areas. Photo points require a camera, film, and local knowledge of photo point location; given these, they are easy to set up and retake. Agencies can encourage participation by external groups or permittees by providing the photographer with film and development. Double prints allow the agency and photographer to keep copies of photographs for their files. Negatives should generally be kept and filed at the agency office.

7. *Video Images* Video cameras, i.e., camcorders, are now available and are able to record multiple images of landscapes for monitoring. While video images provide new ways to record landscape images, limitations in their use should also be considered. Video tapes, especially the quality of the image, may begin to deteriorate within 5 years. These images can be protected by conversion to digital computer images (expensive) or rerecording the original tape onto a new blank tape.

Comparing repeat video images is difficult, especially if the same landscape sequences are not repeated in the same way on subsequent video recordings. Video cameras are also more susceptible to dust and heat damage and cost considerably more than 35-mm cameras. Advantages and disadvantages of video cameras should be carefully considered prior to implementing a video monitoring system.

8. *Repeat Pictures* When repeat pictures are taken, follow the same process used in taking the initial pictures. Include the same area and landmarks in the repeat general view pictures that were included in the initial pictures. Take repeat pictures at approximately the same time of year as the original pictures.

9. *General Observations* General observations concerning the sites on which photographs are taken can be important in interpreting the photos. Such factors as rodent use, insect infestation, animal concentration, fire, vandalism, and other site uses can have considerable impact on vegetation and soil resources. This information can be recorded on note paper or on study method forms themselves if the photographs are taken while collecting other monitoring data.

10. *References*

USDI, Bureau of Land Management. 1985. Rangeland monitoring - Trend studies TR4400-4.

USDA, Forest Service. 1994. Rangeland Analysis and Management Training Guide, Rocky Mountain Region USDA Forest Service Denver, CO.

# Rangeland Monitoring

## Photo Plot Frame - 3- x 3-foot

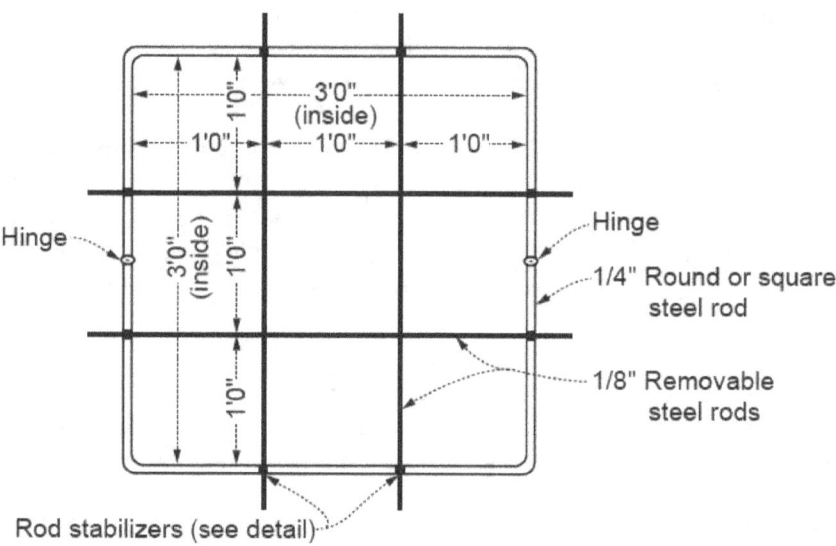

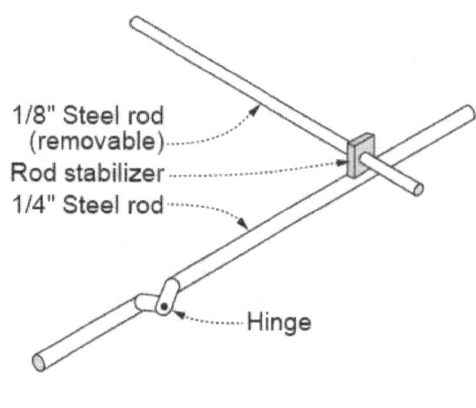

DETAIL

Illustration 1

# Rangeland Monitoring

## Photo Plot Frame—5- x 5-foot

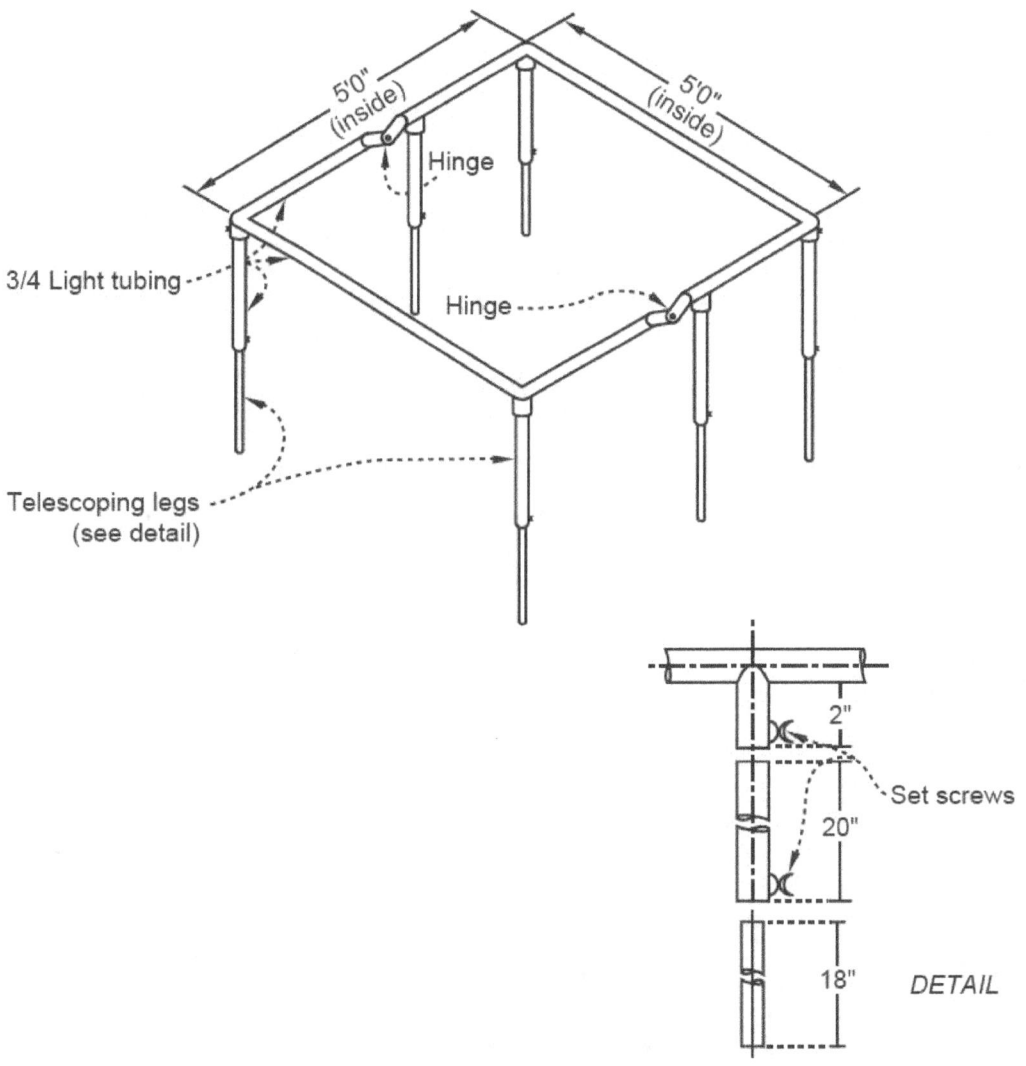

5'0" (inside)

5'0" (inside)

Hinge

Hinge

3/4 Light tubing

Telescoping legs (see detail)

2"

Set screws

20"

18"

*DETAIL*

Illustration 2

35

# Rangeland Monitoring

# Permanent Photo Plot Location

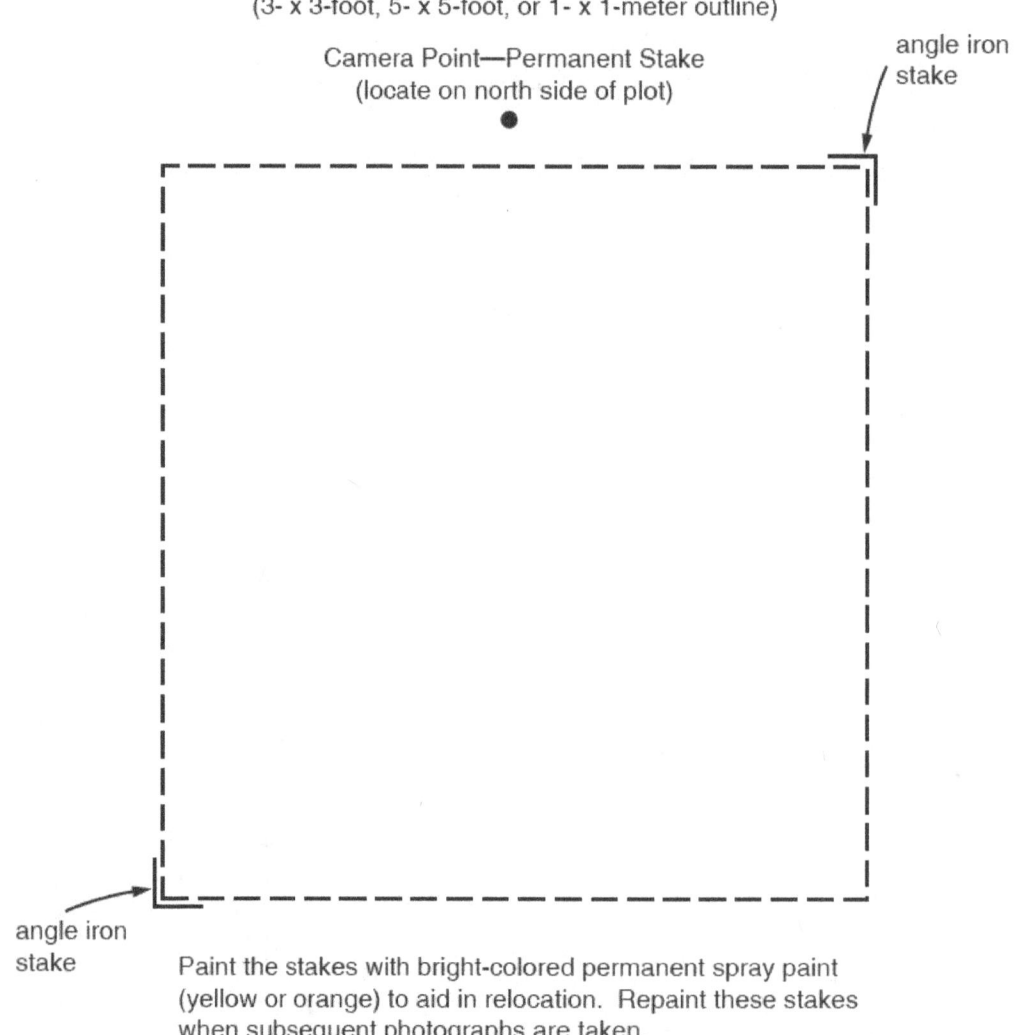

(3- x 3-foot, 5- x 5-foot, or 1- x 1-meter outline)

Camera Point—Permanent Stake
(locate on north side of plot)

angle iron
stake

angle iron
stake

Paint the stakes with bright-colored permanent spray paint
(yellow or orange) to aid in relocation.  Repaint these stakes
when subsequent photographs are taken.

Illustration 3

## B. Frequency Methods - Pace Frequency, Quadrat Frequency, and Nested Frequency Methods

1. *General Description* All three methods consist of observing quadrats along transects, with quadrats systematically located at specified intervals along each transect. The only differences in these technique are the size and configuration of the quadrat frames and the layout of the transect. The following vegetation attributes are monitored with this method:

- Frequency

- Basal cover and general cover categories (including litter)

- Reproduction of key species (if seedling data are collected)

It is important to establish a photo plot (see Section V.A) and take both close-up and general view photographs. This allows the portrayal of resource values and conditions and furnishes visual evidence of vegetation and soil changes over time.

2. *Areas of Use* This method is applicable to a wide variety of vegetation types and is suited for use with grasses, forbs, and shrubs.

3. *Advantages and Limitations*

   a  Frequency sampling is highly objective, repeatable, rapid, and simple to perform, and it involves a minimum number of decisions. Decisions are limited to identifying species and determining whether or not species are rooted within the quadrats (presence or absence).

   b  Frequency data can be collected in different-sized quadrats with the use of the nested frame. When a plant of a particular species occurs within a plot, it also occurs in all of the successively larger plots. Frequency of occurrence for various size plots can be analyzed even though frequency is recorded for only one size plot. This eliminates problems with comparing frequency data from different plot sizes. Use of the nested plot configuration improves the chance of selecting a proper size plot for frequency sampling.

   c  Cover data can also be collected at the same time frequency data is gathered. However, cover data collected in this manner will greatly overestimate cover; unless the tines are honed to a fine point, observer bias will come into play. Another limitation is that the use of one size quadrat will likely result in values falling outside the optimum frequency range (greater than 20 percent to less than 80 percent) for some of the species of interest.

4. *Equipment* The following equipment is needed (see also the equipment list in Section V.A, page 31, for the establishment of the photo plot):

- Study Location and Documentation Data form (see Appendix A)
- Frequency form (see Illustration 4)
- Nested Frequency form (see Illustration 5)
- Permanent yellow or orange spray paint
- Frequency frames (see Illustrations 6 and 7)

- One transect location stake: 3/4 - or 1-inch angle iron not less than 16 inches long
- Hammer
- Tally counter (optional)
- Compass
- Steel post and driver
- Tape: 50-, 100-, or 200-foot delineated in tenths and hundreds or a metric tape of the desired length.

5. *Training* A minimum amount of training is needed for this method. Examiners must be able to identify the plant species and be able to tell whether or not a species occurs, according to study specifications, within a quadrat. Examiners must be familiar with the cover categories and how to collect cover data using the tines on the quadrat frame.

6. *Establishing Studies* Careful establishment of studies is a critical element in obtaining meaningful data (see Section III).

   a **Site Selection** The most important factor in obtaining usable data is selecting representative areas (critical or key areas) in which to run the study (see Sections II.D). Study sites should be located within a single plant community within a single ecological site. Transects and sampling points need to be randomly located within the critical or key areas (see Section III).

   b **Pilot Studies** Collect data on several pilot studies to determine the number of samples (transects or observation points) and the number and size of quadrats needed to collect a statistically valid sample (see Section III.B.8).

   c **Selecting Quadrat Size** The selection of quadrat size is important and depends on the characteristics of the vegetation to be sampled (see Section III.B.6).

      (1) As a rule of thumb, it is expected that all frequency percentages for important species should fall between 10 and 90 percent or, if possible, between 20 and 80 percent. This will provide the greatest possible chance for detecting an important trend for a species when the study is read again. Use a frame size that will produce frequencies falling in this range for the greatest number of species possible.

      (2) To build a sample frame, see Illustration 6, which shows an example of a frequency frame.

      (3) Use the same size quadrat throughout a study and for rereading the study. If frequencies for a specific species approach the extremes of either 0 or 100 percent, it may be necessary to use a different sized quadrat for that species. The nested plot concept would be suitable in this instance.

   d **Nested Plot Technique** The use of one size plot is usually not adequate to collect frequency data on all the important species within a community. For each species occurring on a site, there is a limited range of plot sizes capable of producing frequency percentages between 20 and 80 percent. A plot size appropriate for one species may not be appropriate for another. The nested plot concept is a simple approach to collecting data on two or more different sized plots at one time. Several different sized plots are placed inside each other in a smallest to largest sequence (see Illustration 7).

**e** **Number of Studies** Establish at least one frequency study on each study site; establish more if needed (see Sections II.D and III.B).

**f** **Study Layout** Frequency data can be collected using either the baseline, macroplot, or linear study designs described in Section III.A.2 beginning on page 8. The baseline technique is the one most often used.

Align a tape (100-, or 200-foot, or metric equivalent) in a straight line by stretching it between the baseline beginning stake and the baseline end point stake (see Figure 4 on page 13.) A pin may also be driven into the ground at the midpoint of the transect. Do not allow vegetation to deflect the alignment of the tape. A spring and pulley may be useful to help maintain a straight line.

With the baseline technique, any number of transects can be run perpendicularly to the baseline, depending on the intensity of the sample needed (see Figure 1 on page 9). Each transect originates at a randomly selected mark along the baseline. The randomization is restricted so that half of the transects are randomized on each side of the halfway mark. (Directions for randomly selecting the location of transects to be run off of a baseline using random number tables are given in Appendix D.)

The starting point for each transect off the base line and the distance between each quadrat should not be any closer than the width of the quadrat being used to avoid the possibility that any two quadrats might overlap.

**g** **Reference Post or Point** Permanently mark the location of each study with a reference post and study location stake (see beginning of Section III).

**h** **Study Identification** Number studies for proper identification to ensure that the data collected can be positively associated with specific studies on the ground (see Appendix B).

**i** **Study Documentation** Document pertinent information concerning the study on the Study Location and Documentation Data form (see beginning of Section III and Appendix A).

7. *Taking Photographs* The directions for establishing photo plots and for taking close-up and general view photographs are given in Section V.A.

8. *Sampling Process* In addition to collecting the specific study data, general observations should be made of the study sites (see Section II.F).

**a** **Running the Transect** Study data are collected along several transects. The location of each transect (distance along the baseline) and the direction (to left or right from the baseline) are randomly determined for each study site. A quadrat is read at the specified interval until all quadrats have been read. The interval between quadrats can be either paced or measured. To widen the area transected, add additional paces or distance (20 paces, 50 feet) between quadrats. Additional transects can be added to obtain an adequate sample.

(1)  Start each transect by placing the rear corner of the quadrat frame at the starting point along the baseline tape.

(2)  Place the quadrat frame at the designated interval along a transect perpendicular to the baseline until the specified number of quadrats have been read.  The interval between quadrats can be measured or estimated by pacing.

(3)  When a transect is completed, move to the next starting point on the baseline tape and run the next transect.

b  **Collecting Cover Data**  Record, by dot count tally, the cover category at each of the four corners and at the tip of any tines on the frame.  Enter this data in the Cover Summary section of the Frequency and Nested Frequency forms (see Illustrations 4 and 5).  The cover categories are bare ground (gravel less than 1/12 inch in diameter is tallied as bare ground), litter, and gravel (1/12 inch and larger).  Additional cover categories can be added as needed.  Vegetation is recorded as basal hits or canopy layers in the bottom portion of the form.  Up to three canopy layers can be recorded.  For additional information on collecting vegetation cover data, see Section V.F.8.b on page 72.  Cover data can also be recorded on the Cover Data form, Illustration 13, page 75.

Read the same points on the frame and the same number of points at each placement of the frame throughout a study and when rereading that study.

c  **Collecting Frequency Data**  Collect frequency data for all plant species. Record the data by species within each quadrat using the Frequency form (Illustration 4).  Only one record is made for each species per quadrat, regardless of the number of individual plants of a species that occurs within the quadrat.

(1)  Herbaceous plants (grasses and forbs) must be rooted in the quadrat to be counted.

(2)  On many occasions, rooted frequency on trees and shrubs (including half shrubs) does not provide an adequate sample (occurring within 20% of the plots).  To increase the sample size on trees and shrubs, the canopy overhanging the quadrat can be counted.

(3)  Annual plants are counted whether green or dried.

(4)  Specimens of the plants that are unknown should be collected and marked for later identification.

(5)  Frequency occurrence of seedlings by plant species should be tallied separately from mature plants.

**d Nested Plot Method** Collect frequency data for all plant species. For uniformity in recording data, the four nested plots in a quadrat are numbered from 1 through 4, with the largest plot size corresponding with the higher number. Each time the quadrat frame is placed on the ground, determine the smallest size plot each species occurs in and record the plot number for that quadrat on the Nested Frequency form (Illustration 5).

9. *Calculations* Make the calculations and record the results in the appropriate columns on the Frequency form (see Illustration 4).

    **a Cover** Calculate the percent cover for each cover category by dividing the number of hits for each category by the total number of hits for all categories, including hits on vegetation, and multiplying the value by 100. The total of the percent cover for all cover categories equals 100 percent. Additional information on calculating ground cover, canopy cover, and basal cover can be found in Section F.9 on page 73.

    **b Frequency: Single Plot** On the Frequency form, Illustration 4, total the frequency hits by species. Calculate the percent frequency for each plant species by dividing the total number of hits for that species by the total number of quadrats sampled along the transect and multiplying the value by 100. Record the percent frequency on the form.

    **c Frequency: Nested Plot** Percent frequency by species can be calculated for each transect and/or for the total of all transects.

        (1) *Compiling data* Determine the number of occurrences for each species for each plot size.

            (a) Count the number of occurrences of a species in plot 1 and record the value in the Hits portion of column 1 in the Frequency Summary portion of the Nested Frequency form (see Illustration 5).

            (b) Count the number of occurrences of the same species in plot 2 and add this number to the number recorded for plot 1. Record this total in the Hits portion of column 2.

            (c) Count the number of occurrences of the same species in plot 3 and add this number to the number recorded for plot 2. Record this total in the Hits portion of column 3.

            (d) Count the number of occurrences of the same species in plot 4 and add this number to the number recorded for plot 3. Record this total in the Hits portion of column 4.

        (2) *Frequency for each transect* Calculate the percent frequency of a plant species by plot size for a transect by dividing the number of occurrences by the number of quadrats sampled and multiplying the value by 100. Record in the "% Freq" section of the Frequency Summary portion.

(3) **Total frequency for all transects** Calculate the percent frequency of a plant species by plot size for the total of all transects by adding the occurrences of a species by plot size on all transects, dividing the total by the total number of quadrats sampled for the study, and multiplying the value by 100. Record the percent frequency in the appropriate plot size on a separate form.

10. *Data Analysis* To determine if the change between sampling periods is significant, a Chi Square contingency table analysis should be used. Frequency must be analyzed separately for each species. Chi Square (See Technical Reference, *Measuring & Monitoring Plant Populations*) can also be used to detect changes in cover classes between sampling periods.

11. *References*

Bonham, C.D. 1989. Measurements for Terrestrial Vegetation, John Wiley and Sons, 338 p.

Despain, D.W., P.R. Ogden, and E.L. Smith. 1991. Plant frequency sampling for monitoring rangelands. Some methods for monitoring rangelands and other natural area vegetation. Extension Report 9043. University of Arizona, Tucson, AZ.

Eckert, Richard E., Jr. and John S. Spencer. 1986. Vegetation response on allotments grazed under rest rotation management. Soc. for Range Manage. 39 (2): 166-173.

Francis, Richard E., Richard S. Driscoll, and Jack N. Reppert. 1972. Loop-frequency as related to plant cover, herbage production, and plant density. U.S. Dept. of Agr., For. Ser., Rocky Mtn. For. and Range Exp. Sta., Ft. Collins, CO. Research Paper MA-94. 15 p.

Hironaka, M. 1985. Frequency approaches to monitor rangeland vegetation. Symp. on use of frequency and for rangeland monitoring. William C. Krueger, Chairman. Proc., 38th Annual Meeting, Soc. for Range Manag. Feb. 1985. Salt Lake City, UT. Soc. for Range Manage. 84-86.

Hyder, D.N., C.E. Conrad, P.T. Tueller, L.D. Calvin, C.E. Poulton, and F.A. Sneva. 1963. Frequency sampling of sagebrush-bunchgrass vegetation. Ecology 44:740-746.

Hyder, D.N., R.E. Bement, E.E. Remmenga, and C. Terwilliger, Jr. 1965. Frequency sampling of blue grama range. J. Range Manage. 18:94-98.

Hyder, D.N., R.E. Bement, and C. Terwilliger. 1966. Vegetation-soils and vegetation-grazing relations from frequency data. J. Range Manage. 19:11-17.

Nevada Range Studies Task Group. 1984. Nevada Rangeland Monitoring Handbook. Bureau of Land Management Nevada State Office, Reno, NV. 50 p.

Tueller, Paul T., Garwin Lorain, Karl Kipping, and Charles Wilkie. 1972. Methods for measuring vegetation changes on Nevada rangelands. Agr. Exp. Sta., Univ. of Nevada, Reno, NV. T16. 55 p.

USDI, Bureau of Land Management. 1985. Rangeland monitoring - Trend studies TR4400-4.

West, N.E. 1985. Shortcomings of plant frequency-based methods for range condition and trend. William C. Krueger, Chairman. Proc., 38th Annual Meeting Soc. for Range Manage. Feb. 1985. Salt Lake City. Soc. for Range Manage. 87-90.

Whysong, G.L. and W.W. Brady, 1987. Frequency Sampling and Type II Errors, J. Range Manage. 40:172-174.

# Frequency

| Study Number | Date | Examiner | Allotment Name & Number | Pasture |
|---|---|---|---|---|
| Transect Location | | Number of Quadrats | | Quadrat Size |

## Quadrat Number

| Plant Species | 0 | 10 | 20 | 30 | 40 | 50 | 60 | 70 | 80 | 90 | 100 | Total |
|---|---|---|---|---|---|---|---|---|---|---|---|---|
| | | | | | | | | | | | | |

## Cover Summary

| Vegetation (Basal) | Vegetation (Canopy) | Litter | Bare Ground | Gravel/Stone | |
|---|---|---|---|---|---|
| %Cover | %Cover | %Cover | %Cover | %Cover | %Cover |
| Hits | Hits | Hits | Hits | Hits | Hits |

Notes (use other side or another page)

# Frequency

| Study Number 07N-04W-13-05 | Date 10/27/95 | Examiner Buddy Clump | Allotment Name & Number Blue Dome - 03131 | Pasture |
|---|---|---|---|---|

Transect Location 1 mile East of Weatherby Cattleguard — Number of Quadrats 100 — Quadrat Size 40 × 40 cm

### Quadrat Number

| Plant Species | Total |
|---|---|
| BOGR2 | 65 |
| BOHI2 | 36 |
| PAOB | 6 |
| BOCU | 35 |
| BRRU2 | 10 |
| SIHY | 31 |
| KOCR | 24 |
| VIGUI | 33 |
| HYRI | 16 |
| AMPS | 12 |
| OPUNT | 3 |
| CEGR | 4 |
| ERIOG | 2 |
| PSORA | 3 |
| JUNIP | 1 |

## Cover Summary

| | Vegetation (Basal) | Vegetation (Canopy) | Litter | Bare Ground | Gravel/Stone |
|---|---|---|---|---|---|
| Hits | 20 | 46 | 164 | 136 | 34 |
| %Cover | 5 | 12 | 41 | 34 | 8 |

Notes (use other side or another page)

Illustration 4

# Nested Frequency

| Study Number | Date | Examiner | Allotment Name & Number | Pasture |
|---|---|---|---|---|
| Transect Location | | Number of Quadrats | | Quadrat Size |

**Plant Species** / Quadrats: 1 2 3 4 5 6 7 8 9 10 11 12 13 14 15 16 17 18 19 20

**Frequency Summary by Plot Size**

| | 1 | | 2 | | 3 | | 4 | |
|---|---|---|---|---|---|---|---|---|
| | Hits | % Freq | Hits | % Freq | Hits | % Freq | Hits | % Freq |

**Cover Summary**

| | Hits | %Cover |
|---|---|---|
| Vegetation (Basal) | | |
| Vegetation (Canopy) | | |
| Litter | | |
| Bare Ground | | |
| Gravel/Stone | | |
| Cryptogamic crust | | |

Observations/Comments

Canopy* Dont record ground cover under canopy hits of shrubs under 10ft in height

Notes (Use other side or another page)

Illustration 5

# Nested Frequency

|  |  |
|---|---|
| Study Number | Bear Mountain #1 |
| Date | 10/3/95 |
| Examiner | Rex Allen |
| Allotment Name & Number | Bear Mtn 10205 |
| Pasture | 3 |
| Transect Location | 2 miles north of Roger's well |
| Number of Quadrats | 20 |
| Quadrat Size | 20 |

## Quadrats

| Plant Species | 1 | 2 | 3 | 4 | 5 | 6 | 7 | 8 | 9 | 10 | 11 | 12 | 13 | 14 | 15 | 16 | 17 | 18 | 19 | 20 |
|---|---|---|---|---|---|---|---|---|---|---|---|---|---|---|---|---|---|---|---|---|
| POSE | 1 | 2 | 2 | 2 | 2 | 2 | 2 | 2 | 1 | 2 | 2 | 2 | 2 | 2 | 2 | 1 | 3 | 2 | | 2 |
| SIHY | 2 | 2 | 4 | | | 3 | 3 | 3 | 1 | 2 | 4 | 2 | 3 | 3 | 2 | 3 | 2 | 2 | 4 | 3 |
| PHLO2 | 3 | | 3 | | | | | | 3 | | 1 | 2 | | | 2 | 2 | 2 | 2 | | |
| CHVI8 | 2 | | | | | 4 | 2 | | | | | | | | 4 | | | | | |
| BRTE | 2 | 4 | 3 | 1 | 1 | 2 | 1 | 2 | 1 | 2 | 3 | 2 | 2 | 2 | 2 | 2 | 1 | 2 | 1 | 1 |
| ARTR2 | | 2 | | | | | | 4 | | 2 | 4 | | 3 | | 3 | 4 | | | | |
| ASTRA | | | 3 | | 3 | | | | | | | | | | | | | | | |
| SSSS | | | 4 | | | | | | | | | 4 | | | | | | | | |
| PPFF | | | | | | 3 | | | 4 | | | | | | 4 | | | | | |
| ERIOG | | | | | | | 4 | 4 | | | | 4 | | | | | | | | |
| AAGG | | | | | | | | 4 | | | | | 3 | 4 | | 1 | | | | |
| PHHO | | | | | | | | | | | | | | | 4 | | | | | |

## Frequency Summary by Plot Size

| Plant Species | 1 Hits | 1 % Freq | 2 Hits | 2 % Freq | 3 Hits | 3 % Freq | 4 Hits | 4 % Freq |
|---|---|---|---|---|---|---|---|---|
| POSE | 3 | 8 | 16 | 80 | 17 | 85 | 17 | 85 |
| SIHY | 1 | 5 | 9 | 45 | 15 | 75 | 18 | 90 |
| PHLO2 | 1 | 5 | 5 | 25 | 8 | 40 | 8 | 40 |
| CHVI8 | 0 | 0 | 2 | 10 | 2 | 10 | 4 | 20 |
| BRTE | 7 | 35 | 16 | 80 | 18 | 90 | 19 | 95 |
| ARTR2 | 0 | 0 | 2 | 10 | 4 | 20 | 7 | 35 |
| ASTRA | 0 | 0 | 0 | 0 | 2 | 10 | 2 | 10 |
| SSSS | 0 | 0 | 0 | 0 | 0 | 0 | 2 | 10 |
| PPFF | 0 | 0 | 0 | 0 | 1 | 5 | 3 | 8 |
| ERIOG | 0 | 0 | 0 | 0 | 0 | 0 | 2 | 10 |
| AAGG | 1 | 5 | 1 | 5 | 2 | 10 | 4 | 20 |
| PHHO | 0 | 0 | 0 | 0 | 0 | 0 | 1 | 5 |

## Cover Summary

| Category | Hits | %Cover |
|---|---|---|
| Vegetation (Basal) | 13 | 13 |
| Vegetation (Canopy) | 17 | 17 |
| Litter | 21 | 21 |
| Bare Ground | 31 | 31 |
| Gravel/Stone | 18 | 18 |
| Cryptogamic crust | | |

Observations/Comments

Notes (Use other side or another page)   Canopy* Dont record ground cover under canopy hits of shrubs under 10ft in height

Illustration 5

# Rangeland Monitoring

## Frequency Frame

The frame is made of 3/8-inch
iron rod and 1-inch angle iron
or 1 1/4-inch x 3/16-inch flat iron.

Quadrat size should be based on local conditions
determined from the pilot study.

### QUADRAT

| Number | Size | | Area |
|--------|------|---|------|
| 1 | 7.5 x 7.5 | cm | 56.25 sq cm |
| 2 | 15.0 x 15.0 | cm | 225.00 sq cm |
| 3 | 30.0 x 30.0 | cm | 900.00 sq cm |
| 4 | 40.0 x 40.0 | cm | 1600.00 sq cm |
| 5 | 50.0 x 50.0 | cm | 2500.00 sq cm |
| 6 | 20.0 x 50.0 | cm | 1000.00 sq cm |

40 cm

40 cm

Prong - 1-inch long
1/8-inch wide

The ends of the tines
(both front and rear)
can be tapered to points as
illustrated. These points can
be used to collect additional
cover data.

Illustration 6

# Rangeland Monitoring

## Nested Plot Frame

The frames are made of 3/8-inch
iron rod and 1-inch angle iron
or 1 1/4-inch x 3/16-inch flat iron.
Place tines at the proper intervals
along the rear of the frame and
parallel to the sides to create quadrats
of smaller sizes.

It is convenient to have a 30-, 20-,
15-, 12-, 10-, 6-, and 3-inch quadrat
available.  These different size quadrats
can be combined in three frames.

The 30-inch and 15-inch quadrats can
be combined in one frame.

The 20-inch and 10-inch quadrats can
be combined in one frame.

The 12-inch, 6-inch, and 3-inch quadrats
can be combined in one frame.

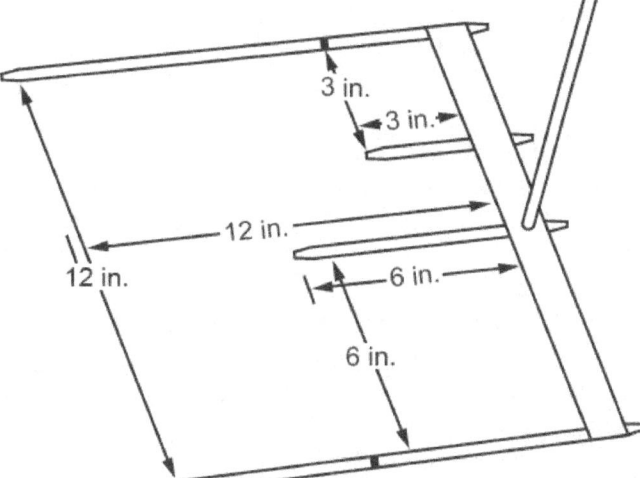

3 in.

3 in.

12 in.

12 in.

6 in.

6 in.

The ends of the tines
(both front and rear)
are tapered to points
as illustrated.  These
points are used to collect
cover data.

Illustration 7

49

## C. Dry Weight Rank Method

1. *General Description* The Dry Weight Rank method is used to determine species composition. It consists of observing various quadrats and ranking the three species which contribute the most weight in the quadrat.

   It is important to establish a photo plot (see Section V.A) and take both close-up and general view photographs. This allows the portrayal of resource values and conditions and furnishes visual evidence of vegetation and soil changes over time.

2. *Areas of Use* This method has been tested in a wide variety of vegetation types and is generally considered suitable for grassland/small shrubs types or understory communities of large shrub or tree communities. It does not work well on large shrubs and trees.

3. *Advantages and Limitations*

   a One advantage of the Dry Weight Rank Method is that a large number of samples can be obtained very quickly. Another advantage is that it deals with estimates of production, which allows for better interpretation of the data to make management decisions. It can be done in conjunction with frequency, canopy cover, or comparative yield methods. Because it is easier to rank the top three species in a quadrat, there is less observer bias.

   b The limitation with this technique is that, by itself, it will not give a reliable estimate of plant standing crop, and it assumes there are few empty quadrats. In many large shrub or sparse desert communities, a high percentage of quadrats are empty or have only one species present. The quadrat size required to address these concerns is often impractical.

4. *Equipment* The following equipment is needed (see also the equipment listed in Section V.A, page 31, for the establishment of the photo plot):

   • Study Location and Documentation Data form (see Appendix A)
   • Dry Weight Rank form (see Illustration 8)
   • Quadrat frame
   • Hammer
   • Permanent yellow or orange spray paint
   • One stake: 3/4 - or 1-inch angle iron not less than 16 inches long
   • Compass
   • Steel post and driver

5. *Training* Examiners must be able to identify the plants. Experience in weight estimate is desirable, but those with experience must break the habit of assigning percentages and just rank the species, as well as not debating over the close calls. The large number of sampling units tends to reduce the problems with close calls.

6. *Establishing Studies*

   a **Site Selection** The most important factor in obtaining usable data is selecting representative areas (critical or key areas) in which to run the study (see Section II.D).  Study sites should be located within a single plant community within a single ecological site.  Transects and sampling points need to be randomly located within the critical or key areas (see Section III).

b **Pilot Studies**  Collect data on several pilot studies to determine the number of samples (transects or observation points) and the number and size of quadrats needed to collect a statistically valid sample (see Section III.B.8).

c **Selecting Quadrat Size**  Adapt the size and shape of quadrats to the vegetation community to be sampled.

    (1)  Select a plot size on the premise that most plots should contain three species.

    (2)  Determine the proper size quadrat to use by doing preliminary sampling with different size frames (see Illustration 6).

    (3)  Use the same size quadrat throughout a study and for rereading the study.  If frequencies approach the extremes of either 0 or 100 percent, it may be necessary to change the quadrat size.

d **Number of Studies**  At least one Dry Weight Rank study should be established on each study site, depending on the objectives; establish more if needed (see Sections II.D and III.B).  Evaluate the rangeland plant communities where studies will be located and determine the number of transects and quadrats needed.  The purpose is to collect the best possible sample for the greatest number of species in any plant community.

e **Study Layout**  The Dry Weight Rank data can be collected using the baseline, macroplot, or linear study designs described in Section III.A.2 beginning on page 8.  The linear technique is the one most often used.

f **Reference Post or Point**  Permanently mark the location of each study with a reference post and a study location stake (see beginning of Section III).

g **Study Identification**  Number studies for proper identification to ensure that the data collected can be positively associated with specific sites on the ground (see Appendix B).

h **Study Documentation**  Document pertinent information concerning the study on the Study Location and Documentation Data form (see beginning of Section III and Appendix A).

7. *Taking Photographs*  The directions for establishing photo plots and for taking close-up and general view photographs are given in Section V.A.

8. *Sampling Process*  In addition to collecting the specific study data, general observations should be made of the study sites (see Section II.F).

Determine the transect bearing and select a prominent distant landmark such as a peak, rocky point, etc., that can be used as the transect bearing point.

After the quadrat location has been determined, the observer decides which three species in the quadrat have the greatest yield of current year's growth on a dry matter basis. The species with the highest yield is given a rank of 1, the next 2, and the third highest a 3. Data are record by quadrat on the Dry Weight Rank form, Illustration 8. All other species present are ignored. If there are not three species present in the quadrat, a multiple rank is assigned.

The Dry Weight Rank method assumes that a rank of 1 corresponds to 70% composition, rank 2 to 20%, and rank 3 to 10%. If only one species is found in a quadrat, it would be ranked 1, 2 and 3 (100%). If two species are found, one may be given ranks of 1 and 2 (90%), ranks 1 and 3 (80%), or ranks 2 and 3 (30%), depending on the relative weight for the two species (see Illustration 8). For each species, record the number of 1, 2, or 3 ranks received in the sample.

Data can also be collected and recorded for each quadrat for use in conjunction with the Comparative Yield Method.

9. *Calculations*

   a  For each species multiply the number of ranks of 1, 2, and 3 by 7, 2, and 1, respectively, and record under the appropriate weight column. Add the amounts in the weight columns of each species and record in the weighted column.

   b  Total the weighted column for all species. The total of this column will always be ten times the number of quadrats.

   c  Divide the value recorded for each species in the weighted column by the total of the weighted column to get percent composition for each species. Percent composition, by definition, should total 100 percent.

10. *Data Analysis*  Chi Square analysis can be used to determine if the frequency of each species in each rank tally group (1,2, or 3) has changed from one sampling period to another. Each species must be analyzed separately.

11. *References*

   Despain, D.W., P.R. Ogden, and E.L. Smith. 1991. Plant frequency sampling for monitoring rangelands. In: G.B. Ruyle, ed. Some Methods for Monitoring Rangelands and other Natural Area Vegetation. Extension Report 9043, University of Arizona, College of Agriculture, Tucson, AZ.

# Dry Weight Rank

| Study Number | | Date | | Examiner | | Allotment Name & Number | | Pasture | |
|---|---|---|---|---|---|---|---|---|---|
| Transect Location | | | | | | Number of Quadrats | | Quadrat Size | |

| Species | Quadrat | | | | | | | | | | | | | | | | | | | | Rank Tally | | | Weighted | % Comp. |
|---|---|---|---|---|---|---|---|---|---|---|---|---|---|---|---|---|---|---|---|---|---|---|---|---|---|
| | 1 | 2 | 3 | 4 | 5 | 6 | 7 | 8 | 9 | 10 | 11 | 12 | 13 | 14 | 15 | 16 | 17 | 18 | 19 | 20 | 1 | 2 | 3 | | |
| | | | | | | | | | | | | | | | | | | | | | | | | | |
| | | | | | | | | | | | | | | | | | | | | | | | | | |
| | | | | | | | | | | | | | | | | | | | | | | | | | |
| | | | | | | | | | | | | | | | | | | | | | | | | | |
| | | | | | | | | | | | | | | | | | | | | | | | | | |
| | | | | | | | | | | | | | | | | | | | | | | | | | |

Observations/Comments

Illustration 8

# Dry Weight Rank

|  |  |
|---|---|
| Study Number | Eagle Creek #1 |
| Date | 8/16/95 |
| Examiner | Joe Smith |
| Allotment Name & Number | Eagle Creek 1010 |
| Pasture | 1 |
| Transect Location | 3 miles west of Border Tank |
| Number of Quadrats | 20 |
| Quadrat Size | 40 cm × 40 cm |

| Species | 1 | 2 | 3 | 4 | 5 | 6 | 7 | 8 | 9 | 10 | 11 | 12 | 13 | 14 | 15 | 16 | 17 | 18 | 19 | 20 | Rank Tally 1 | Rank Tally 2 | Rank Tally 3 | Weighted | % Comp. |
|---|---|---|---|---|---|---|---|---|---|---|---|---|---|---|---|---|---|---|---|---|---|---|---|---|---|
| BOER4 | 1 | 1 | 2 | 2 | 1 | 2 |  | 2 | 1 |  | 1 |  | 1 | 1 |  |  |  | 2 | 1 |  | 8 | 5 | 2 | 68 | 34 |
| HILE |  |  | 1 | 1 | 3 | 1 |  |  | 3 |  | 2 |  |  | 2 |  | 3 | 2 | 1 |  |  | 4 | 5 | 6 | 44 | 22 |
| BOGR |  | 3 | 3 | 3 |  | 3 | 1 | 1 | 3 | 1 | 3 | 2 | 3 | 3 | 1 | 1 | 3 |  | 3 | 3 | 4 | 1 | 6 | 36 | 18 |
| BOCU |  | 2 |  | 3 |  |  | 2 | 3 | 2 | 2 |  | 1 |  |  | 2 |  | 3 | 3 | 2 | 2 | 1 | 6 | 1 | 20 | 10 |
| LUPIN | 3 |  |  |  | 2 |  | 3 | 3 |  | 3 | 3 | 3 |  |  |  |  | 1 |  |  | 1 | 0 | 2 | 5 | 9 | 5 |
| HAGR |  |  |  |  |  |  |  |  |  |  |  |  | 2 |  |  |  |  |  |  | 1 | 3 | 1 | 0 | 23 | 11 |

Observations/Comments:

Illustration 8

# D. Daubenmire Method

1. *General Description* The Daubenmire method consists of systematically placing a 20- x 50-cm quadrat frame along a tape on permanently located transects (see Figure 4 on page 13). The following vegetation attributes are monitored using the Daubenmire method:

   - Canopy cover
   - Frequency
   - Composition by canopy cover

   It is important to establish a photo plot (see Section V.A) and take both close-up and general view photographs. This allows the portrayal of resource values and conditions and furnishes visual evidence of vegetation and soil changes over time.

2. *Areas of Use* This method is applicable to a wide, variety of vegetation types as long as the plants do not exceed waist height.

3. *Advantages and Limitations* This method is relatively simple and rapid to use. A limitation is that there can be large changes in canopy cover of herbaceous species between years because of climatic conditions, with no relationship to the effects of management. In general, quadrats are not recommended for estimating cover (Floyd and Anderson 1987; Kennedy and Addision 1987). This method cannot be used to calculate rooted frequency.

4. *Equipment* The following equipment is needed (see also the equipment listed in Section V.A, page 31, for the establishment of the photo plot):

   - Study Location and Documentation Data form Appendix A)
   - Daubenmire forms (see Illustration 9 and 10)
   - Hammer
   - Permanent yellow or orange spray paint
   - Two stakes: 3/4 - or 1-inch angle iron not less than 16 inches long
   - Tape: 100- or 200-foot, delineated in tenths and hundreds, or a metric tape of the desired length.
   - Steel pins (reinforcement bar) for marking zero, mid, and end points of the transect
   - Frame to delineate the 20- x 50-cm quadrats (see Illustration 11)
   - Compass
   - Steel post and driver

5. *Training* The accuracy of data depends on the training and ability of the examiners. Examiners must be able to identify the plant species. They must receive adequate and consistent training in laying out transects and making canopy coverage estimates using the frame.

6. *Establishing Studies* Careful establishment of studies is a critical element in obtaining meaningful data (see Section III).

   a **Site Selection** The most important factor in obtaining usable data is selecting representative areas (critical or key areas) in which to run the study (see Section II.D). Study sites should be located within a single plant community within a single ecological site. Transects and sampling points need to be randomly located within the critical or key areas (see Section III).

b **Pilot Studies** Collect data on several pilot studies to determine the number of samples (transects or observation points) and the number and size of quadrats needed to collect a statistically valid sample (see Section III.B.8).

c **Number of Studies** Establish a minimum of one study on each study site; establish more if needed (see Section II.D and III.B).

d **Study Layout** Data can be collected using the baseline, macroplot, or linear study designs described in Section III.A.2 beginning on page 8. The linear technique is the one most often used.

(1) Align a tape (100-, or 200-foot, or metric equivalent) in a straight line by stretching it between the transect location and the transect bearing stakes. Do not allow vegetation to deflect the alignment of the tape. A spring and pulley may be useful to maintain a straight line. The tape should be aligned as close to the ground as possible.

(2) Drive steel pins almost to the ground surface at the zero point on the tape and at the end of the transect. A pin may also be driven into the ground at the midpoint of the transect. (see Figure 4 on page 13)

e **Reference Post or Point** Permanently mark the location of each study with a reference post and a study location stake (see beginning of Section III).

f **Study Identification** Number studies for proper identification to ensure that the data collected can be positively associated with specific sites on the ground (See Appendix B).

g **Study Documentation** Document pertinent information concerning the study on the Study Location and Documentation Data form (see beginning of Section III and Appendix A).

7. *Taking Photographs* The directions for establishing photo plots and for taking close-up and general view photographs are given in Section V.A.

8. *Sampling Process* In addition to collecting the specific studies data, general observations should be made of the study sites (see Section II.F).

a **Cover Classes** This method uses six separate cover classes (Daubenmire 1959). The cover classes are:

| Cover Class | Range of Coverage | Midpoint of Range |
|---|---|---|
| 1 | 0 - 5% | 2.5% |
| 2 | 5 - 25% | 15.0% |
| 3 | 25 - 50% | 37.5% |
| 4 | 50 - 75% | 62.5% |
| 5 | 75 - 95% | 85.0% |
| 6 | 95 - 100% | 97.5% |

b **Ten Cover Classes** Where narrower and more numerous classes are preferred, a ten-cover class system can be used.

c **Collecting Cover Data** As the quadrat frame is placed along the tape at the specified intervals, estimate the canopy coverage of each plant species. Record the data by quadrat, by species, and by cover class on the Daubenmire form (see Illustration 9). Canopy coverage estimates can be made for both perennial and annual plant species.

(1) Observe the quadrat frame from directly above and estimate the cover class for all individuals of a plant species in the quadrat as a unit. All other kinds of plants are ignored as each plant species is considered separately.

(2) Imagine a line drawn about the leaf tips of the undisturbed canopies (ignoring inflorescence) and project these polygonal images onto the ground. This projection is considered "canopy coverage." Decide which of the classes the canopy coverage of the species falls into and record on the form.

(3) Canopies extending over the quadrat are estimated even if the plants are not rooted in the quadrat.

(4) Collect the data at a time of maximum growth of the key species.

(5) For tiny annuals, it is helpful to estimate the number of individuals that would be required to fill 5% of the frame (the 71- x 71-mm area). A quick estimate of the numbers of individuals in each frame will then provide an estimate as to whether the aggregate coverage falls in Class 1 or 2, etc.

(6) Overlapping canopy cover is included in the cover estimates by species; therefore, total cover may exceed 100 percent. Total cover may not reflect actual ground cover.

9. *Calculations* Make the calculations and record the results in the appropriate columns on the Daubenmire form (see Illustrations 9 and 10).

a **Canopy Cover** Calculate the percent canopy cover by species as follows:

(1) On the Daubenmire form (Illustration 9) count the number of quadrats in each of the six cover class (by species) and record in the Number column on the Daubenmire Summary form (Illustration 10).

(2) Multiply this value times the midpoint of the appropriate cover class (Illustration 10).

(3) Total the products for all cover classes by species.

(4) Divide the sum by the total number of quadrats sampled on the transect.

(5) Record the percent cover by species on the form.

b **Frequency** Calculate the percent frequency for each plant species by dividing the number of occurrences of a plant species (the number of quadrats in which a plant species was observed) by the total number of quadrats sampled along the transect. Multiply the resulting value by 100. Record the percent frequency on the form (Illustration 10).

c **Species Composition** With this method, species composition is based on canopy cover of the various species. It is determined by dividing the percent canopy cover of each plant species by the total canopy cover of all plant species. Record the percent composition on the form (Illustration 10).

10. *Data Analysis* Tests should be directed at detecting changes in cover of the species and/or in major ground cover classes. Tests for changes in minor species will have low power to detect change. If quadrats are spaced far enough apart on each transect so as to be considered independent, the quadrat can be analyzed as the sampling unit. Otherwise, the transects should be considered the sampling units. If the transects are treated as the sampling unit, and given that the transects are permanent, either the paired t-test or the nonparametric Wilcoxon signed rank test should be used to test for change between two years. Repeated measures ANOVA can be used to test for differences between 3 or more years. If the quadrats are treated as the sampling units, care must be taken to ensure they are positioned the same along each transect in each year of measurement. A paired t-test, Wilcoxon signed rank test, or ANOVA is then used as described above for transects.

11. *References*

Daubenmire, Rexford. 1959. A Canopy-coverage method of vegetational analysis. Northwest Science 33:43-64.

———— 1968. Plant communities: a textbook of plant synecology. Harper and Row, New York. 300 p.

USDI, Bureau of Land Management. 1985. Rangeland monitoring - Trend Studies TR4400-4.

# Daubenmire

| Study Number | Date | Examiner | Allotment Name & Number | Pasture |
|---|---|---|---|---|

Transect Number and Location

Number of Quadrats

## Quadrat

| Plant Species | 1 | 2 | 3 | 4 | 5 | 6 | 7 | 8 | 9 | 10 | 11 | 12 | 13 | 14 | 15 | 16 | 17 | 18 | 19 | 20 | 21 | 22 | 23 | 24 | 25 |
|---|---|---|---|---|---|---|---|---|---|---|---|---|---|---|---|---|---|---|---|---|---|---|---|---|---|
| | | | | | | | | | | | | | | | | | | | | | | | | | |
| | | | | | | | | | | | | | | | | | | | | | | | | | |
| | | | | | | | | | | | | | | | | | | | | | | | | | |
| | | | | | | | | | | | | | | | | | | | | | | | | | |
| | | | | | | | | | | | | | | | | | | | | | | | | | |
| | | | | | | | | | | | | | | | | | | | | | | | | | |
| | | | | | | | | | | | | | | | | | | | | | | | | | |
| | | | | | | | | | | | | | | | | | | | | | | | | | |

## Quadrat

| Plant Species | 26 | 27 | 28 | 29 | 30 | 31 | 32 | 33 | 34 | 35 | 36 | 37 | 38 | 39 | 40 | 41 | 42 | 43 | 44 | 45 | 46 | 47 | 48 | 49 | 50 |
|---|---|---|---|---|---|---|---|---|---|---|---|---|---|---|---|---|---|---|---|---|---|---|---|---|---|
| | | | | | | | | | | | | | | | | | | | | | | | | | |
| | | | | | | | | | | | | | | | | | | | | | | | | | |
| | | | | | | | | | | | | | | | | | | | | | | | | | |
| | | | | | | | | | | | | | | | | | | | | | | | | | |
| | | | | | | | | | | | | | | | | | | | | | | | | | |
| | | | | | | | | | | | | | | | | | | | | | | | | | |
| | | | | | | | | | | | | | | | | | | | | | | | | | |
| | | | | | | | | | | | | | | | | | | | | | | | | | |

**Illustration 9**

# Daubenmire

| Study Number | Date | Examiner | Allotment Name & Number | Pasture |
|---|---|---|---|---|
| 035-27W-08-02 | 7/24/95 | Chuck Wagon | Quaking Aspen – 10373 | Sheep Creek |

Transect Number and Location: 3 miles north of Eagle Creek on the west side of the road

Number of Quadrats: 50

## Quadrat

| Plant Species | 1 | 2 | 3 | 4 | 5 | 6 | 7 | 8 | 9 | 10 | 11 | 12 | 13 | 14 | 15 | 16 | 17 | 18 | 19 | 20 | 21 | 22 | 23 | 24 | 25 |
|---|---|---|---|---|---|---|---|---|---|---|---|---|---|---|---|---|---|---|---|---|---|---|---|---|---|
| AGSP | 2 | | 1 | | 2 | | | | 1 | | | | 2 | | | 3 | | 4 | | | | | 3 | 1 | |
| PONE | 1 | | | | | 2 | 3 | | | | | | | | | | | | 4 | | 1 | | | 2 | |
| ORHY | | 3 | | 1 | | | | | | | | | | | | | | | | | | | | | |
| STTH2 | | | | | 1 | | | | | 3 | | | | | | | | | | | | | | | |
| SIHY | | | | | | | | 1 | | | | | | | | | | | | | | | 1 | | |
| BRTE | | | | | | | | | | 1 | | 1 | | | | | | | | | | | | 1 | |
| PHHO | | | | | | | | | | | | | | 2 | | | | | | 1 | | 1 | 2 | | |
| CRAC 2 | | | | | | | | | | | | 1 | | | | | | | | | | 1 | | | |
| ASTER | | | | | | | | | | | | 2 | | | | | | | | | 1 | | | | |
| ARTR 2 | | | | | | | | | | | | | | 3 | 3 | | | 4 | | | | 4 | | | |
| CHVI 8 | | | | | | | | | | | | | 4 | | | | | | | | | | | 3 | |

## Quadrat

| Plant Species | 26 | 27 | 28 | 29 | 30 | 31 | 32 | 33 | 34 | 35 | 36 | 37 | 38 | 39 | 40 | 41 | 42 | 43 | 44 | 45 | 46 | 47 | 48 | 49 | 50 |
|---|---|---|---|---|---|---|---|---|---|---|---|---|---|---|---|---|---|---|---|---|---|---|---|---|---|
| AGSP | | | 1 | | | | | | | 1 | 2 | | | | 1 | | | | 1 | | | 1 | 1 | | |
| PONE | | | | | | | | 2 | | | 1 | | | 1 | 3 | | | 2 | | | 1 | | | | |
| ORHY | | | | | | 1 | | | | | | | | | | | | | | 1 | | | | 1 | |
| STTH2 | | | | | 3 | | | | 4 | | | 4 | | | | | | | | | 2 | | | | |
| SIHY | | | | | 1 | | | | | | | | | | | | | | | | | | | | |
| BRTE | | | | | | | | | | | | 1 | 2 | | | | | | | | | | 1 | | |
| PHHO | | | | | | | 1 | | | | | | | | | 1 | | | | | | | 1 | | |
| ASTER | | | | | | | 1 | 1 | | | 2 | | | | | | | | | | | | | | |
| ARTR 2 | | 4 | | 3 | | | | | | | 4 | | | 2 | | | | | 2 | | | 2 | | | |
| CHVI 8 | | | | 3 | | | | 5 | | | | | | | | 2 | | | 4 | | | | | | |

# Daubenmire Summary

Study Number ___ | Date ___ | Examiner ___ | Allotment Name & Number ___ | Pasture ___

Study Location ___

Number of Quadrats ___

| Cover Class | Mid-Point | Species — Product | Species — Number | Species — Product | Species — Number | Species — Product | Species — Number | Species — Product | Species — Number | Species — Product | Species — Number | Species — Product | Species — Number | Species — Product | Species — Number | Species — Product | Species — Number | Species — Product | Species — Number | Species — Product | Species — Number |
|---|---|---|---|---|---|---|---|---|---|---|---|---|---|---|---|---|---|---|---|---|---|
| 1  1-5% | 2.5 | | | | | | | | | | | | | | | | | | | | |
| 2  5-25% | 15 | | | | | | | | | | | | | | | | | | | | |
| 3  26-50% | 37.5 | | | | | | | | | | | | | | | | | | | | |
| 4  51-75% | 62.5 | | | | | | | | | | | | | | | | | | | | |
| 5  76-95% | 85 | | | | | | | | | | | | | | | | | | | | |
| 6  96-100% | 97.5 | | | | | | | | | | | | | | | | | | | | |
| Total canopy | | | | | | | | | | | | | | | | | | | | | |
| Number of Samples | | | | | | | | | | | | | | | | | | | | | |
| % canopy cover | | | | | | | | | | | | | | | | | | | | | |
| Species composition | | | | | | | | | | | | | | | | | | | | | |
| Frequency | | | | | | | | | | | | | | | | | | | | | |

Illustration 10

61

# Daubenmire Summary

| Study Number | Date | Examiner | Allotment Name & Number | Pasture |
|---|---|---|---|---|
| 035-27W-08-02 | 7/24/95 | Chuck Wagon | Quaking Aspen 11037 | Sheep Creek |

Study Location: Three miles north of Eagle Tank on the west side of road.

Number of Quadrats: 50

| Cover Class | Mid-Point | AGSP Number | AGSP Product | PONE Number | PONE Product | ORHY Number | ORHY Product | STTH2 Number | STTH2 Product | SIHY Number | SIHY Product | BRTE Number | BRTE Product | PHHO Number | PHHO Product | CRAC2 Number | CRAC2 Product | Aster Number | Aster Product | ARTR2 Number | ARTR2 Product | CHIV8 Number | CHIV8 Product |
|---|---|---|---|---|---|---|---|---|---|---|---|---|---|---|---|---|---|---|---|---|---|---|---|
| 1  1-5% | 2.5 | 10 | 25 | 5 | 12.5 | 2 | 5 | 3 | 7.5 | 2 | 5 | 6 | 15 | 4 | 10 | 3 | 7.5 | 3 | 7.5 | 1 | 2.5 | | |
| 2  5-25% | 15 | 5 | 75 | 3 | 45 | | | 1 | 15 | | | 1 | 15 | 2 | 30 | | | 2 | 30 | 2 | 30 | 2 | 30 |
| 3  26-50% | 37.5 | 2 | 75 | 2 | 75 | 1 | 37.5 | 2 | 75 | | | | | | | | | | | 2 | 75 | 3 | 112.5 |
| 4  51-75% | 62.5 | 1 | 62.5 | 1 | 62.5 | | | | | | | | | | | | | | | 6 | 375 | 2 | 125 |
| 5  76-95% | 85 | | | | | | | | | | | | | | | | | | | | | 1 | 85 |
| 6  96-100% | 97.5 | | | | | | | | | | | | | | | | | | | | | | |
| Total canopy | | | 237.5 | | 195 | | 42.5 | | 97.5 | | 5 | | 30 | | 40 | | 7.5 | | 37.5 | | 482.5 | | 352.5 |
| Number of Samples | | | 50 | | 50 | | 50 | | 50 | | 50 | | 50 | | 50 | | 50 | | 50 | | 50 | | 50 |
| % canopy cover | | | 5 | | 4 | | 1 | | 2 | | 1 | | 1 | | 1 | | 1 | | 1 | | 10 | | 7 |
| Species composition | | | 16 | | 13 | | 3 | | 6 | | 1 | | 3 | | 3 | | 1 | | 3 | | 31 | | 22 |
| Frequency | | | 36 | | 22 | | 6 | | 12 | | 4 | | 14 | | 12 | | 6 | | 10 | | 22 | | 16 |

Illustration 10

# Rangeland Monitoring

## Daubenmire Frame

Six Cover Class Frame

The frame is made of 3/8-inch iron rod. The inside dimensions of the frame are 20 x 50 centimeters. The frame should have sharpened legs 3 centimenters long welded to each corner to help hold the frame in place.

The six cover class frame is divided into fourths by painting alternate sections of the frame different colors as illustrated. Use orange and white or red and white paint.

In one corner of the frame, delineate two sides of an area 71 millimeters square as illustrated. This area represents 5% of the quadrat area.

The painted design provides visual reference areas equal to 5, 25, 50, 75, 95, and 100% of the plot area.

**Illustration 11**   63

## E. Line Intercept Method

1. *General Description*  The Line Intercept method consists of horizontal, linear measurements of plant intercepts along the course of a line (tape). It is designed for measuring grass or grass-like plants, forbs, shrubs, and trees. The following vegetation attributes are monitored with this method:

   - Foliar and basal cover
   - Composition (by cover)

   It is important to establish a photo plot (see Section V.A) and take both close-up and general view photographs. This allows the portrayal of resource values and conditions and furnishes visual evidence of vegetation and soil changes over time.

2. *Areas of Use*  This method is ideally suited for semiarid bunchgrass-shrub vegetation types.

3. *Advantages and Limitations*  The Line Intercept method is best suited where the boundaries of plant growth are relatively easy to determine. It can be adapted to sampling varying densities and types of vegetation. It is not well adapted, however, for estimating cover on single-stemmed species, dense grassland situations, litter, or gravel less than 1/2 inch in diameter. It is best suited to estimating cover on shrubs.

4. *Equipment*  The following equipment is needed (see also the equipment listed in Section V.A, page 31, for the establishment of the photo plot):

   - Study Location and Documentation Data form (see Appendix A)
   - Line Intercept form (see Illustration 12)
   - Hammer
   - Permanent yellow or orange spray paint
   - Two stakes: 3/4 - or 1-inch angle iron not less than 16 inches long.
   - Two tapes: 100- or 200-foot, delineated in tenths and hundredths, or a metric tape of the desired length
   - Compass
   - Steel post and driver

5. *Training*  A minimum of training is needed to make sure the examiners understand how to lay out baselines and transects and how to make the measurements. The examiner must also be able to identify the plant species.

6. *Establishing Studies*  Careful establishment of studies is a critical element in obtaining meaningful data (see Section III).

   a  **Site Selection**  The most important factor in obtaining usable data is selecting representative areas (critical or key areas) in which to run the study (see Section II.D). Study sites should be located within a single plant community within a single ecological site. Transects and sampling points need to be randomly located within the critical or key areas (see Section III).

**b Pilot Studies** Collect data on several pilot studies to determine the number of samples (transects or observation points) and the number and size of quadrats needed to collect a statistically valid sample (see Section III.B.8).

**c Number of Transects** Establish the minimum number of transects to achieve the desired level of precision for the key species in each study site (see Section III.B).

**d Length of Transect** The length of a transect is based on the density and homogeneity of the vegetation. If the vegetation is sparse, a longer transect is needed. Transects may be any length (eg. 100 feet, 200 feet, or even longer).

**e Study Layout** Line Intercept data can be collected using either the baseline or linear study design described in Section III.A.2 beginning on page 8. The baseline technique is the recommended study design.

(1) The study location stake is placed at the beginning of the baseline. After determining the bearing of the study, a stake is placed at the end of the baseline. Transects are run perpendicular to and at random distances along the baseline. Transect location stakes are placed at the beginning and end of each transect. The distance between the stakes dependents on the length of the transect. The height of the stakes depends on the height of the vegetation. (Directions for randomly selecting the location of transects to be run off of a baseline using random number tables are given in Appendix D).

Transect location stakes may be left in place as permanent markers or removed at the conclusion of the study. Permanently marking transects will result in greater power to detect change.

(2) Stretch the transect tapes between stakes as close to the ground as possible, with the zero point of the tape aligned on the baseline (the beginning point of the transect). Do not allow vegetation to deflect the alignment of the tape.

**f Reference Post or Point** Permanently mark the location of each study with a reference post and a study location stake (see beginning of Section III).

**g Study Identification** Number studies for proper identification to ensure that the data collected can be positively associated with specific sites on the ground. (see Appendix B).

**h Study Documentation** Document pertinent information concerning the study on the Study Location and Documentation Data form (see beginning of Section III and Appendix A).

7. *Taking Photographs* The directions for establishing photo plots and for taking close-up and general view photographs are given in Section V.A.

8. *Sampling Process* In addition to collecting the specific studies data, general observations should be made of the study sites (see Section II.F).

Proceed down the tape stretched along the transect line and measure the horizontal linear length of each plant that intercepts the line. Measure grasses and grass-like plants, along with rosette-forming plants, at ground level. For forbs, shrubs, and trees, measure the vertical projection of the foliar cover intercepting one side of the tape. Be sure not to inadvertently move the tape to include or exclude certain plants. If the measurements are made in 10ths and 100ths of feet, the totals are easily converted to percentages. The measurements are recorded by species on the Line Intercept form (Illustration 12).

9. *Calculations* Make the calculations and record the results on the Line Intercept form (see Illustration 12).

   **a Cover**

   (1)  Calculate the percent cover of each plant species by totaling the intercept measurements for all individuals of that species along the transect line and convert this total to a percent.

   (2)  Where the measurements are made in 10ths and 100ths of feet along a 100-foot transect, the totals for each species are the cover percentages.

   (3)  Calculate the total cover measured on the transect by adding the cover percentages for all the species. This total could exceed 100% if the intercepts of overlapping canopies are recorded.

   **b Composition** With this method, species composition is based on the percent cover of each species. Calculate percent composition by dividing the percent cover for each plant species by the total cover for all plant species.

10. *Data Analysis* It is important to realize that each transect is a single sampling unit. For trend analysis permanent sampling units are suggested. If permanent transects are monitored, use the appropriate paired analysis technique. Use either a paired t-test or the nonparametric Wilcoxon signed rank test when testing for change between years. When comparing more than two sampling periods, use repeated measures ANOVA. If the transects are not permanently marked, use the appropriate nonpaired test.

11. *References*

Brun, Jorge M. and Thadis W. Box. 1963. Comparison of line intercepts and random point frames for sampling desert shrub vegetation. J. Range Manage. 16:21-25.

Buckner, D.L. 1985. Point-Intercept Sampling in Revegetation Studies: Maximizing Objectivity and Repeatability. Paper presented at American Society for Surface Mining and Reclamation Meeting, Denver, CO. 1985.

Canfield, R.H. 1941. Application of the line interception method in sampling range vegetation. J. Forestry 39:388-394.

Canfield, R.H. 1944. Measurement of grazing use by the line intercept Method. Jour. For. 42(3):192-194

Hanley, Thomas A. 1978. A comparison of the line-interception and quadrat estimation methods of determining shrub canopy coverage. J. Range Manage. 31:60-62.

Kinsinger, Floyd E., Richard E. Eckert, and Pat 0. Currie. 1960. A comparison of the line-interception, variable-plot, and loop methods as used to measure shrub-crown cover. J. Range Manage. 13:17-21.

USDI, Bureau of Land Management. 1985. Rangeland monitoring - Trend studies TR4400-4.

# Line Intercept

| Study Number | Date | Examiner | Allotment Name & Number | Pasture |
|---|---|---|---|---|
| Line Length | | Transect Location | | |

| | | Totals | | | 100% |
|---|---|---|---|---|---|
| **Shrub Species** | NOTES | | | | |
| **Forb Species** | | | | | |
| **Grass Species** | | | | | |
| NOTES (Use other side or another page, if necessary) | Totals | | | | |
| | % Cover | | | | |
| | % Comp | | | | |

Illustration 12

# Line Intercept

| Study Number 12N-37W-19-03 | Date 10/3/95 | Examiner Jack Straw | Allotment Name & Number Cow Gulch 20111 | Pasture |
|---|---|---|---|---|

Line Length 100 feet  
Transect Location 3 miles east of Potter's Corral on north side of road.

**NOTES** (Use other side or another page, if necessary)

100 ft. tape

| | Grass Species | | | | | Forb Species | | | Shrub Species | | NOTES |
|---|---|---|---|---|---|---|---|---|---|---|---|
| | BOCU | BOGR2 | BOHI2 | KOCR | SIHY | HYRI | PSORA | COWR2 | CEGR2 | JUNIP | |
| | .42 | .10 | .32 | .11 | .06 | .52 | 2.04 | .55 | 3.40 | .06 | |
| | .20 | .02 | .25 | .02 | .02 | .46 | 1.32 | .22 | .13 | 2.13 | |
| | .26 | .03 | .05 | .12 | .02 | 1.47 | .59 | | 4.90 | .07 | |
| | .03 | .01 | | .08 | .04 | .28 | 3.30 | | .72 | .02 | |
| | .17 | .10 | | | .05 | .80 | .07 | | .14 | | |
| | .26 | .39 | | | .26 | .05 | | | 1.02 | | |
| | .22 | .24 | | | .04 | | | | | | |
| | .22 | .14 | | | .03 | | | | | | |
| | .34 | .10 | | | .01 | | | | | | |
| | .32 | .17 | | | .19 | | | | | | |
| | .02 | .12 | | | .02 | | | | | | |
| | .02 | .18 | | | .35 | | | | | | |
| | .10 | .13 | | | | | | | | | |
| | .02 | .14 | | | | | | | | | |
| | .16 | .04 | | | | | | | | | |
| | | .16 | | | | | | | | | |
| | | .05 | | | | | | | | | |
| | | .27 | | | | | | | | | |
| | | .03 | | | | | | | | | |
| | | .46 | | | | | | | | | |
| | | .07 | | | | | | | | | |
| | | .38 | | | | | | | | | |
| | | .12 | | | | | | | | | |
| | | .10 | | | | | | | | | |
| | | .02 | | | | | | | | | |
| | | .11 | | | | | | | | | |
| | | .03 | | | | | | | | | |
| | | .03 | | | | | | | | | |
| | | .02 | | | | | | | | | |
| | | .36 | | | | | | | | | |
| | | .68 | | | | | | | | | |
| **Totals** | 3.64 | 4.63 | .62 | .33 | 1.09 | 3.58 | 7.32 | .77 | 10.31 | 2.28 | **Totals** 100% |
| **% Cover** | 4 | 5 | 1 | 0 | 1 | 4 | 7 | 1 | 10 | 2 | |
| **% Comp** | 11 | 14 | 3 | — | 3 | 11 | 20 | 3 | 29 | 6 | |

Illustration 12 — 69

# F. Step-Point Method

1. *General Description* The Step-Point Method involves making observations along a transect at specified intervals, using a pin to record cover "hits." It measures cover for individual species, total cover, and species composition by cover.

   It is important to establish a photo plot (see Section V.A) and take both close-up and general view photographs. This allows the portrayal of resource values and conditions and furnishes visual evidence of vegetation and soil changes over time.

2. *Areas of Use* This method is best suited for use with grasses and forbs, as well as low shrubs. The greater the structure to the community, the more difficult it becomes to determine "hits" due to parallax, observer bias, wind, etc. This method is good for an initial overview of an area not yet subjected to intensive monitoring.

3. *Advantages and Limitations* This method is relatively simple and easy to use as long as careful consideration is given to the vegetation type to which it is applied. It is suitable for measuring major characteristics of the ground and vegetation cover of an area. Large areas can easily be sampled, particularly if the cover is reasonably uniform. It is possible to collect a fairly large number of samples within a relatively short time.

   A limitation of this method is that there can be extreme variation in the data collected among examiners when sample sizes are small. Tall or armored vegetation reduces the ability to pace in a straight line, and the offset for obstructions described in the procedures adds bias to the data collection by avoiding certain components of the community. Another limitation is that less predominant plant species may not be hit on the transects and therefore do not show up in the study records. The literature contains numerous studies utilizing point intercept procedures that required point densities ranging from 300 to 39,000 in order to adequately sample for minor species. One major consideration in the use of this method is to assure that a sharpened pin is used and that only the point is used to record "hits." Pins have finite diameters and therefore overestimate cover (Goodall 1952). Another limitation of this method is that statistical analysis of the data is suspect unless two and preferably more transects are run per site (see Section III - Study Design and Analysis).

4. *Equipment* The following equipment is needed (see also the equipment listed in Section V.A, page 31, for the establishment of the photo plot):

   - Study Location and Documentation Data form (see Appendix A)
   - Cover Data form (see Illustration 13)
   - Permanent yellow or orange spray paint
   - Tally counter (optional)
   - One stake: 3/4- or 1-inch angle iron not less than 16 inches long
   - 3-foot long, 3/16th-inch diameter sharpened pin
   - Compass
   - Steel post and driver

5. *Training* A minimum amount of training is needed for this method. Examiners must be able to identify the plant species, be familiar with the ground-level cover

categories, know how to collect canopy or foliar cover data, and know how to collect cover data using a pin and notch in the boot.

6. *Establishing Studies* Careful establishment of studies is a critical element in obtaining meaningful data.

   a **Site Selection** The most important factor in obtaining usable data is selecting representative areas (critical or key areas) in which to run the study (see Section II.D). Study sites should be located within a single plant community within a single ecological site. Transects and sampling points need to be randomly located within the critical or key areas. (see Section III).

   b **Pilot Studies** Collect data on several pilot studies to determine the number of samples (transects or observation points) and the number and size of quadrats needed to collect a statistically valid sample (see Section III.B.8).

   c **Number of Transects** Establish the minimum number of transects to achieve the desired level of precision (see Section III.B).

   d **Study Layout** Data can be collected using either the baseline or linear study designs described in Section III.A.2 beginning on page 8. The linear technique is the one most often used.

   e **Reference Post or Point** Permanently mark the location of each study with a reference post and a study location stake (see beginning of Section III).

   f **Study Identification** Number studies for proper identification to ensure that the data collected can be positively associated with specific sites on the ground (see Appendix B).

   g **Study Documentation** Document pertinent information concerning the study on the Study Location and Documentation Data form (see beginning of Section III and Appendix A).

7. *Taking Photographs* The directions for establishing photo plots and for taking close-up and general view photographs are given in Section V.A.

8. *Sampling Process* In addition to collecting the specific studies data, general observations should be made of the study sites (see Section II.F).

   a **Running a Transect** Determine the transect bearing and select a prominent distant landmark such as a peak, rocky point, etc., that can be used as the transect bearing point.

   (1) Start a transect by randomly selecting a point along the transect bearing and reading the first hit (observation point).

   (2) Read hits at specified intervals by placing the heel of the boot on the ground with the sole of the boot at a 30-degree angle to the ground. Place the pin into the 3/16th inch wide by 1/8th inch deep notch in the toe of

the boot and vertically lower the pin until it either intersects an herbaceous plant or the ground for the specified number of hits. It is recommended that the interval be a minimum of 5 paces. To lengthen the transect, increase the distance between hits (10 paces, 20 paces, etc.).

(3) When obstructions such as juniper trees, cholla cactus, or ledge rock, etc., are encountered, sidestep at 90° from the transect line and continue pacing parallel to the transect to avoid the obstructions. Return to the original transect line as soon as possible by sidestepping at 90° in the opposite direction. Continue pacing along the transect bearing. If the obstruction (juniper tree, cholla cactus, or ledge rock) is determined to be a highly important component of the community, this information can be recorded qualitatively on the back of the form.

(4) In most cases, do not count hits along portions of a transect that have been unnaturally disturbed, such as roads or trails. When such areas are encountered, proceed three paces past the disturbance before resuming the reading of hits along the transect line.

b **Collecting Cover Data** At each observation point, identify the ground level or basal hit with the point of the pin and record the data by dot count tally by category and/or plant species code in the appropriate section of the Cover Data form (see Illustrations 13 and 14). If there is a vegetation canopy layer, lower the pin through the vegetation until a basal or ground level hit is determined. Record the basal or ground level hit and any subsequent vegetation layers that intersect the pin. For vegetation structure above 3-feet (length of pin), a visual observation of plant intercepts above the notch in the boot can be made and recorded as additional canopy or foliar level hits on the data form.

(1) *Ground-level or basal hits*

(a) Ground-level hits (excluding basal vegetation hits) will fall into four cover categories. They can be redefined and/or additional categories added, depending on the data needed. The four categories are:

L - Litter

B - Bare ground

G - Gravel (particle sizes between 1/12 inch and 10 inches)

S - Stone (greater than 10 inches)

(b) Record the ground-level hits by dot count tally by ground-level cover category in the Ground-Level Cover section of the form, except where there are ground-level and, basal or canopy cover hit combinations. In this situation, use the Basal and Canopy/Foliar Cover section of the form.

(c) Basal hits on live vegetation are identified by species (includes mosses and lichens more than 1/16 inch thick). To count as a basal hit on live vegetation, the plant crown at or below a 1-inch height above the ground MUST be intercepted by the pin.

(d) Enter the appropriate plant species code in the Basal or Ground-Level Column in the Basal and Canopy/Foliar Cover section of the form.

(e) Enter a dot count tally for each basal hit on a species in the Dot Count Column in the Basal and Canopy/Foliar Cover section of the form when the plant species code is first entered on the form. Enter an additional dot count tally each time there is a basal hit on that species on the transect, except where there are basal and canopy/foliar cover hit combinations.

(2) ***Ground-level or basal and canopy/foliar cover hit combinations***

(a) Identify the ground-level or basal hit, as well as any canopy cover hit(s) below 3 feet in height, intercepted at each point by the pin. For canopy cover above 3 feet, use line-of-sight observations directly perpendicular to the notch in the boot.

(b) Enter the appropriate ground-level cover category code and/or plant species code for each level of hit (up to four levels) in the appropriate columns in the Basal and Canopy/Foliar Cover section of the form (see Illustration 13).

(c) Enter a dot count tally for each ground-level or basal and canopy/foliar cover hit combination when it is first entered on the form and each time this same combination is encountered on the transect.

(d) Enclose plant species codes for vegetation cover hits more than 20 feet above ground level in brackets [ ].

9. *Calculations* Calculate the percent cover for each cover category by dividing the number of hits for each category by the total number of hits for all categories, including hits on vegetation.

   a **Ground Cover** Ground cover is determined by dividing the total number of hits for all categories except bare ground by the total number of hits (including bare ground).

   b **Canopy/Foliar Cover** Canopy/Foliar cover is determined by dividing the total number of hits on vegetation (includes all basal and canopy/foliar hits) by the total number of hits.

   c **Basal Cover** Basal cover is determined by dividing the number of basal hits by the total number of hits.

10. *Data Analysis*

   a When transects are the sampling units: For trend analysis, permanent sampling units are suggested. If permanent transects are monitored, use the appropriate paired analysis technique to compare change in average cover by species and cover class. When comparing more than two sampling periods, use repeated measures ANOVA. If the transects are not permanently marked, use the appropriate nonpaired test.

**b** When points are the sampling units: To determine if the change between sampling periods is significant, use Chi Square analysis of variance for cover data.

## 11. References

Bonham, C.D. 1989. Measurements for Terrestrial Vegetation, John Wiley and Sons, New York, NY. 338 p.

Evans, Raymond A. and R. Merton Love. 1957. The step-point method of sampling—a practical tool in range research. J. Range Manage. 10:208-212.

Goodall, D.W. 1952. Some considerations in the use of point quadrats for the analysis of vegetation. Aust. J. Sci. Res., Series B 5:1-41

Mueller-Dombois, Dieter and Heinz Ellenberg. 1974. Aims and methods of vegetation ecology. John Wiley & Sons, New York, NY. 547 p.

USDI, Bureau of Land Management. 1985. Rangeland monitoring - Trend studies TR4400-4.

## Cover Data

| Study Number | | Date | Examiner | | Pasture |
|---|---|---|---|---|---|
| Allotment Name & Number | | Study Location | | | Number of Points |

### Ground-Level Cover

| Category | **B** Bare Ground | **L** Litter | **G** Gravel (2mm-10") | **S** Stone (>10") | Vegetation | Total |
|---|---|---|---|---|---|---|
| Dot Count | | | | | | |
| Total Hits | | | | | | |
| % Cover | | | | | | |

### Basal and Canopy/Foliar Cover

| Bsl or Grnd-Lev | Level 1 | Level 2 | Level 3 | Dot Count | Total Hits |
|---|---|---|---|---|---|
| | | | | | |
| | | | | | |
| | | | | | |
| | | | | | |
| | | | | | |
| | | | | | |
| | | | | | |
| | | | | | |
| | | | | | |
| | | | | | |
| | | | | | |
| | | | | | |
| | | | | | |
| | | | | | |
| | | | | | |
| | | | | | |
| | | | | | |
| | | | | | |
| | | | | | |
| | | | | | |
| | | | | Total | |

Notes (use other side or another page)

Illustration 13     75

## Cover Data

| Study Number Red Feather #2 | Date 9/28/95 | Examiner Josh Gibson | Pasture 1 |
|---|---|---|---|

| Allotment Name & Number Red Feather 11473 | Study Location Two miles south of Headquarters Well on west side of road. | Number of Points 100 |
|---|---|---|

### Ground-Level Cover

| Category | B Bare Ground | L Litter | G Gravel (2mm-10") | S Stone (>10") | Vegetation | Total |
|---|---|---|---|---|---|---|
| Dot Count | ▨ | ▨ : | ▨ ⊡ : | : | | 39 |
| Total Hits | 9 | 12 | 16 | 2 | 61 | 100 |
| % Cover | 9 | 12 | 16 | 2 | 61 | 100 |

### Basal and Canopy/Foliar Cover

| Bsl or Grnd-Lev | Level 1 | Level 2 | Level 3 | Dot Count | Total Hits |
|---|---|---|---|---|---|
| L | BOCU | | | ▨ : | 12 |
| G | BOGR 2 | D | [ JUNIP ] | • | 1 |
| BOGR 2 | Junip | | | ▨ ▨ | 20 |
| G | BOCU | | | • • | 4 |
| SIHY | | | | • | 2 |
| L | ERIOG | | | • | 2 |
| G | SIHY | RHTR | | • | 2 |
| B | VIGUI | | | • | 2 |
| G | L | VIGUI | | • • | 4 |
| B | BOCU | | | • | 2 |
| B | BOHI 2 | | | • • | 3 |
| L | BOGR 2 | BOCU | | • | 2 |
| BOCU | L | | | • | 2 |
| OPUNT | | | | • | 1 |
| BOGR 2 | BOCU | | | • | 2 |
| | | | | | |
| | | | | | |
| | | | | | |
| | | | | | |
| | | | | | |
| | | | | Total | 61 |

Notes (use other side or another page)

Illustration 13

## Diagrammatic Sketches of Sample Units (Hits) and Recording Procedures

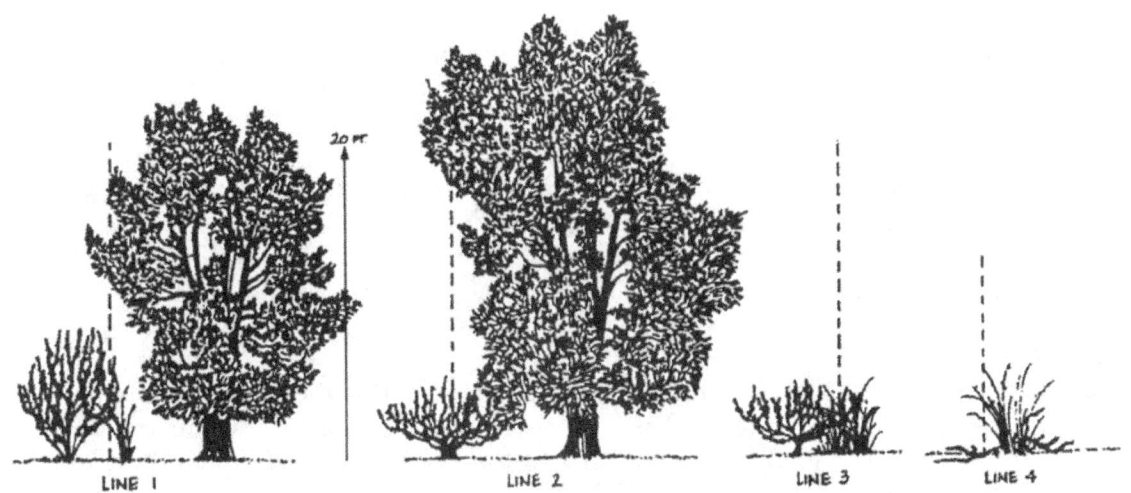

The data from the above illustrated sample units (hits) are recorded on the Cover Data Form as follows:

| | BASAL and FOLIAR | | | |
|---|---|---|---|---|
| | BSL or grnd-lev | Foliar-level 1 | Foliar-level 2 | Foliar-level 3 |
| Line 1 — | B | AGSP | PUTR 2 | PIED |
| Line 2 — | ARTR 2 | [PIED] | | |
| Line 3 — | AGSP | CHNA 2 | | |
| Line 4 — | L | AGSP | | |
| | | | | |
| | | | | |
| | | | | |

Note — To count as a basal hit on live vegetation, the plant crown at or below a 1-inch height above the ground must be intercepted by the pin.

— Dead vegetation in the canopy is counted as litter.

— Enclose plant species codes for vegetation cover hits more than 20 feet above ground level in brackets [ ].

Illustration 14                77

## G. Point-Intercept Method - Sighting Devices, Pin Frames, and Point Frames

1. *General Description* The Point-Intercept method consists of employing a sighting device or pin/point frame along a set of transects to arrive at an estimate of cover. It measures cover for individual species, total cover, and species composition by cover.

   It is important to establish a photo plot (see Section V.A) and take both close-up and general view photographs. This allows the portrayal of resource values and conditions and furnishes visual evidence of vegetation and soil changes over time.

2. *Areas of Use* This method is suited to all vegetation types less than about 1.5 meters in height. This is because sighting devices and pin/point frames require the observer to look down on the vegetation from above in a vertical line with the ground. If the sighting device allows upward viewing, the method can also be used to estimate the canopy cover of large shrubs and trees.

3. *Advantages and Limitations* Point interception measurements are highly repeatable and lead to more precise measurements than cover estimates using quadrats. The method is more efficient than line intercept techniques, at least for herbaceous vegetation, and it is the best method of determining ground cover and the cover of the more dominant species. Given the choice between sighting devices and pin/point frames, the optical sighting device is preferable.

   A limitation of point-intercept sampling is the difficulty in picking up the minor species in the community without using a very large number of points. In addition, wind will increase the time required to complete a study because of the need to view a stationary plant.

   One limitation that is specific to the use of point frames is that a given number of points grouped in frames gives less precise estimates of cover than the same number of points distributed individually (Goodall 1952; Greig-Smith 1983). In fact, single-pin measurements require only one-third as many points as when point frames are used (Bonham 1989). Another problem with frames is that they overestimate the cover of large or clumped plants because the same plant is intercepted by different points on the same frame (Bonham 1989). This problem is overcome with the method described here by treating the frames as the sampling units (rather than using the individual points as sampling units). However, this approach doesn't change the fact that more points must be read than when the points are independent.

   Use of a pin frame device (as opposed to a grid frame made of crossing strings) will result in overestimation of cover because the pins have finite diameter. The use of a sharpened pin will greatly reduce overestimation when only the point of the pin is used to record a hit or a miss.

4. *Equipment* The following equipment is needed (see also the equipment listed in Section V.A, page 31, for the establishment of the photo plot):

   - Study Location and Documentation Data form (see Appendix A)
   - Cover Data form (see Illustration 13 on page 75)
   - Sighting device (see Illustration 15)[4]

---

[4] A sighting device is available commercially from ESCO, P.O. Box 18775, Boulder, Colorado 80308.

- Tripod for mounting sighting device
- Panhead for tripod (makes possible rapid positioning of sighting device)
- Pin or point frame. This can be a pin frame (see Illustration 16), usually with 10 pins (Bonham 1989; Pieper 1973) or a point frame (see Illustration 17), consisting of two superimposed string grids mounted one above the other on three adjustable legs (Floyd and Anderson 1983). The design of Floyd and Anderson (1983) produces a sighting grid of 36 points per frame.
- Hammer
- Permanent yellow or orange spray paint
- Tally counter (optional)
- Two stakes: 3/4 - or 1-inch angle iron not less than 16 inches long
- Compass
- Steel post and driver
- Tape: 50-, 100-, or 200-foot delineated in tenths and hundreds or a metric tape of the desired length.

5. *Training* A minimum of training is needed to make sure the examiners understand how to lay out baselines and transects and position and read the specific sighting device or pin/point frame being employed. The examiners must also be able to identify the plant species.

6. *Establishing Studies* Careful establishment of studies is a critical element in obtaining meaningful data.

   a **Site Selection** The most important factor in obtaining usable data is selecting representative areas (critical or key areas) in which to run the study (see Section II.D). Study sites should be located within a single plant community within a single ecological site. Transects and sampling points need to be randomly located within the critical or key areas (see Section III).

   b **Pilot Studies** Collect data on several pilot studies to determine the number of samples (transects or observation points) and the number and size of quadrats needed to collect a statistically valid sample (see Section III.B.8).

   c **Study Layout** Data can be collected using either the baseline or linear study designs described in Section III.A.2 beginning on page 8. The baseline technique is the recommended procedure.

   d **Reference Post or Point** Permanently mark the location of each study with a reference post and a study location stake (see beginning of Section III).

   e **Study Identification** Number studies for proper identification to ensure that the data collected can be positively associated with specific sites on the ground (see Appendix B).

   f **Study Documentation** Document pertinent information concerning the study on the Study Location and Documentation Data form (see beginning of Section III and Appendix A).

7. *Taking Photographs* The directions for establishing photo plots and for taking close-up and general view photographs are given in Section V.A.

8. *Sampling Process* In addition to collecting the specific studies data, general observations should be made of the study sites (see Section II.F).

a **Transects** Run a series of transects perpendicular to the baseline in both directions. The beginning points for each transect are randomly selected points along the baseline and the direction of each transect is also randomly determined (see Section III.A.2).

To ensure that both transects and points/point frames are independent, spacing between transects and between points/point frames on each transect should be greater than the average diameter of the largest plants likely to be sampled. (If only basal cover is to be sampled, this diameter is the basal diameter; otherwise, it is canopy diameter.)

b **Sampling along Transects** The first point/point frame read on each transect should be randomly determined. After the first point/point frame is read, all others are spaced the predetermined interval from the first point. If a tape is used for the transects, always read on the same side of the tape.[5]

- *Sighting Device* Determine hits by sighting through the device and recording the cover category in the cross hairs.

- *Pin/point frames* Determine hits by recording the cover category intercepted by each of the points. For pin frames, this is the cover category hit by each pin; for grid frames, this is the cover category determined by sighting through the "cross hairs" formed by each of the intersections of strings.

Hits are recorded on the Cover Data form (Illustration 13) in the following categories: vegetation (by plant species), litter, gravel, stone, and bare ground. Prior to recording data, the examiner needs to determine if canopy/foliar cover or basal cover (or both) will be recorded and if hits will be recorded in more than one canopy layer. For sighting devices and some pin/point frames, recording hits in more than one canopy layer requires that upper layers be temporarily moved out of the way to provide a direct line of sight to the lower canopy layers.

c **Paired Samples** If the data are to be analyzed as paired samples, each transect should be permanently marked the first year at both ends. In each subsequent year of measurement, a tape should be run from one end to the other and the points/point frames read at the selected intervals along the transect. This process should then be repeated for each transect.

d **Independent Samples** If the data are to be analyzed as independent samples, the transects do not have to be permanently marked. In this case, it is sufficient to pace each transect, taking measurements at each specified pace interval. The observer must ensure, however, that no bias is introduced by subconsciously "choosing" the point to be read. Such bias can be avoided by looking at the horizon when placing the tripod down.

---

[5] One of the devices manufactured by ESCO employs a mounting arm that is exactly 0.5 m long from tripod pivot to the axis of point projection. With this device, two points along each transect can be read with each placement of the tripod (assuming that 1 m is the selected interval between points). If this device is used, the tripod is placed at 2 m intervals along the tape (or at a number of paces approximating 2 m if no tape is used), the arm is rotated toward the baseline, the intercepted object is recorded, the arm rotated 180°, the next intercepted object is recorded, and so on.

9. *Calculations* Make the calculations and record the results on the Cover Data form (see Illustration 13, page 75).

   a **Cover of Individual Plants, Litter, Gravel, Stone, and Bare Ground**

   (1) *Paired samples* Calculate the percent cover of each species along *each* transect by totaling all of the "hits" for that species along the transect, dividing the hits by the total number of points along the transect, and multiplying by 100. Calculate the total percent cover for the species in the sampled area by adding together all the transect cover values for the species and dividing by the number of transects. Do the same for litter, gravel, stone, and bare ground.

   When point frames are used, the point frames themselves can be analyzed as sampling units. In this case, percent cover of each species is calculated for each point frame. Percent cover is calculated by totaling all of the "hits" for that species in one frame, dividing the hits by the total number of points in that frame, and multiplying by 100. In this situation, cover data for each frame must be recorded separately on one form or on separate forms.

   (2) *Independent samples: Sighting device and pin frames* Calculate the percent cover of each species in the study area as a whole by totaling all the "hits" for that species along all of the transects, dividing by the total number of points in the study, and multiplying by 100. Do the same for litter, gravel, stone, and bare ground.

   (3) *Independent samples: Point frames* For independent samples, the frames themselves can be considered the sampling units. Calculate the percent cover of each species in each point frame by totaling all the "hits" for that species in the frame, dividing the hits by the total number of points in the frame, and multiplying by 100. Calculate the total percent cover for the species in the sampled area by adding together all of the point frame cover values for the species and dividing by the number of point frames. Do the same for litter, gravel, stone, and bare ground.

   (4) *Total vegetation cover* Calculate total vegetation cover by adding the study area cover percentages for all plant species. This total could exceed 100 percent if multiple hits (overlapping canopies) were recorded at each point along the transect.

   b **Species Composition** Species composition is based on the percent cover of the various species. Calculate percent composition by dividing the percent cover for each plant species by the total cover for all plant species.

10. *Data Analysis* The method of data analysis depends upon whether or not the transects are permanent.

   a **Permanent Transects** If the transects are permanent, the transects or point frames are the sampling units. Either a paired t test or the nonparametric Wilcoxon signed rank test is used to test for significant change in average cover between two sampling periods. Repeated measures analysis of variance is used to test for significant change in average cover between three or more sampling periods.

**b Transects Not Permanent** If the transects are not permanent, that is, if they are randomly located in each sampling period, then the samples are independent and the points can be treated as the sampling units.

Sighting Devices: Analysis consists of a Chi Square contingency table analysis to test for significant change between years in numbers of "hits" on the key species, other plant species, or cover classes.

Point Frames: Analysis consists of testing for significant changes in average cover between sampling periods using the independent sample $t$ test or the nonparametric Mann Whitney U test. Independent sample analysis of variance or the nonparametric Kruskal-Wallis test is used to test for significant changes in average cover between three or more years.

## 11. References

Bonham, C.D. 1989. Measurements for Terrestrial Vegetation, John Wiley and Sons, 338 p.

Brown, Dorothy. 1954. Methods of surveying and measuring vegetation. Commonwealth Bureau of Pastures and Field Crops. Bulletin No. 42. Commonw. Agr. Bur., Farmham Royal, Bucks, England. 223 p.

Brun, Jorge M. and Thadis W. Box. 1963. Comparison of line intercepts and random point frames for sampling desert shrub vegetation. J. Range Management. 16:21-25.

Buckner, D.L. 1985. Point-intercept sampling in revegetation studies; maximizing objectivity and repeatability. Proceedings of the American Society of Surface Mining and Reclamation. 1985 Annual Meeting, Denver, CO.

Goodall, D.W. 1952. Some considerations in the use of point quadrats for the analysis of vegetation. Aust. J. Sci. Res., Series B 5:1-41

Greig-Smith, P. 1983. Quantitative plant ecology. 3rd Ed. University of California Press Berkeley and Los Angeles.

Floyd, D.A., and J.E. Anderson. 1983. A new point interception frame for estimating cover of vegetation. Idaho National Engineering Laboratory Radioecology and Ecology Programs 1983 Progress Report, pp.107-113

Levy, E.B. and E.A. Madden. 1933. The Point method for Pasture Analysis. New Zealand J. Agric. 46: 267-279.

Mueller-Dombois, Dieter and Heinz Ellenberg. 1974. Aims and methods of vegetation ecology. John Wiley & Sons, New York. 547 p.

Stanton, F.W. 1960. Ocular Point Frame. J. Range Manage. 13:153.

Winkworth, R.E. and D.W. Goodall. 1962. A Crosswire Sighting Tube for Point-Quadrat Analysis. Ecology 43:342-343.

## Examples of Sighting Devices

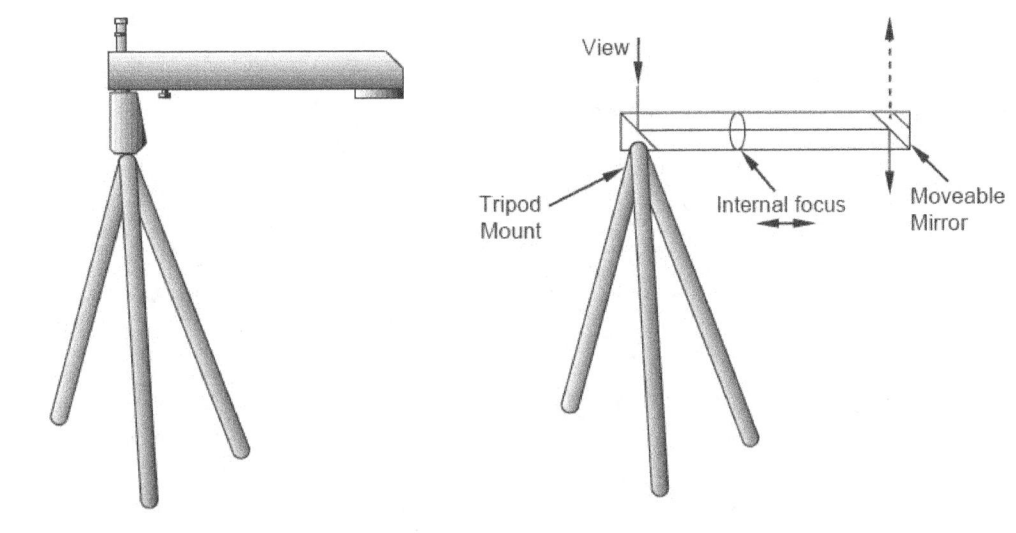

Illustration 15

83

# Examples of Pin Frames

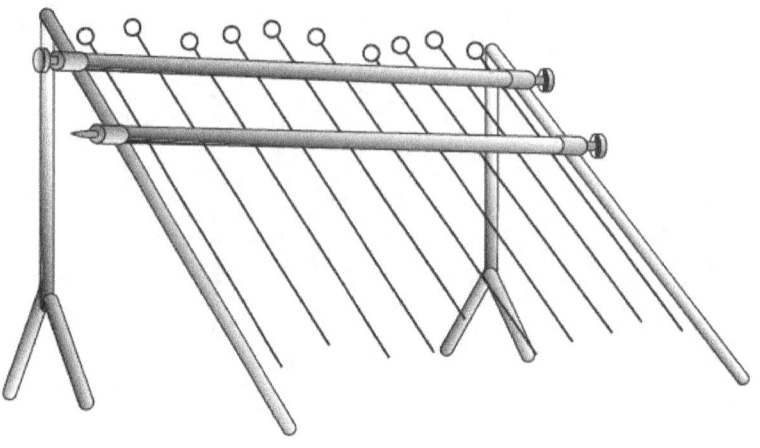

Illustration 16

## Example of a Point Frame

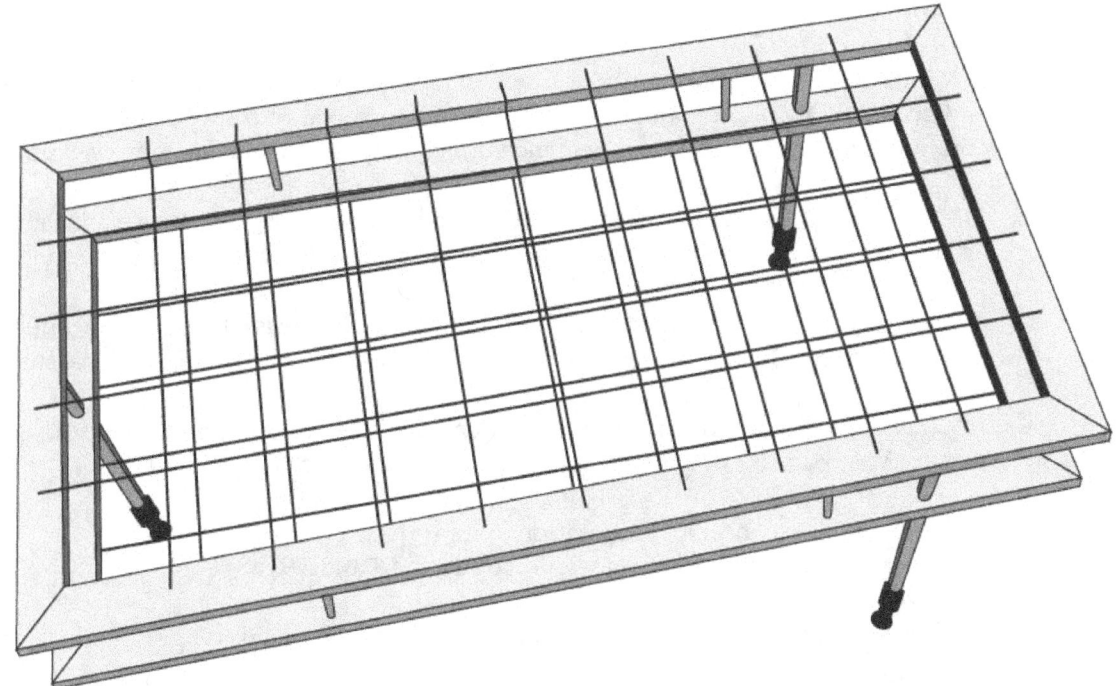

Illustration 17

85

# H. Cover Board Method

1. *General Description*  The Cover Board method uses a profile board or density board to estimate the vertical area of a board covered by vegetation from a specified distance away. This technique is designed to evaluate changes in the vegetation structure over time. Quantifying the vegetation structure for statistical comparison was described by Nudds (1977). The following vegetation attributes are monitored using this method:

   - Vertical cover
   - Structure

   It is important to establish a photo plot (see Section V.A) and take both close-up and general view photographs. This allows the portrayal of resource values and conditions and furnishes visual evidence of vegetation and soil changes over time.

2. *Areas of Use*  This method is applicable to a wide variety of vegetation types. It should be used with those that show potential for changes, such as woody riparian vegetation.

3. *Advantages and Limitations*  The Cover Board technique is a fast and easily duplicated procedure. The size of the board can be modified to meet the purpose of the study.

4. *Equipment*  The following equipment is needed (see also the equipment listed in Section V.A, page 31, for the establishment of the photo plot):

   - Study Location and Documentation Data form (Appendix A)
   - Cover Board Method forms (see Illustrations 18 and 19)
   - Cover board (see Illustration 20)
   - One stake: 3/4- or 1-inch angle iron not less than 16 inches long
   - Hammer
   - Permanent yellow or orange spray paint
   - Compass
   - Steel post and driver

5. *Training*  The accuracy of the data depends on the training and ability of the examiners. They must receive adequate and consistent training in laying out transects. A minimum of training is needed to make sure the examiners understand how to position the cover board and estimate percent cover. Examiners must also be able to identify plant species if estimates are to be made be species.

6. *Establishing Studies*  Careful establishment of studies is a critical element in obtaining meaningful data (see Section III).

   a **Site Selection**  The most important factor in obtaining usable data is selecting representative areas (critical or key areas) in which to run the study (see Section II.D). Study sites should be located within a single plant community within a single ecological site. Transects and sampling points need to be randomly located within the critical or key areas (see Section III).

   b **Pilot Studies**  Collect data on several pilot studies to determine the number of samples (transects or observation points) and the number and size of quadrats needed to collect a statistically valid sample (see Section III.B.8).

c **Number of Transects** Establish the minimum number of transects to achieve the desired level of precision for the key species in each study site (see Section III.B).

d **Study Layout** Data can be collected using either the baseline or linear study designs described in Section III.A.2 beginning on page 8. The linear technique is the most often used procedure.

(1) *Linear transect*

(a) Determine the transect bearing and select a prominent distant land-mark such as a peak, rocky point, etc., that can be used as the transect bearing point.

(b) Randomly select an observation point along the transect. The cover board will be placed 15 feet from this observation point in a random direction. One way to select a random direction is by using the second hand on a standard watch. Look at the watch and note the direction the second hand is pointing. Another way is to randomly select a three digit number between 0 and 360 from a random number table to represent the degrees on a compass (see Appendix D for directions and a table of random digits). After taking the initial reading, remain at the observation point on the transect and take three additional readings at 90-degree angles from the original bearing and at the same distance (15 feet). Additional observation points can be established at specified intervals from the initial observation point along the transect bearing. A piece of angle iron or rebar should be placed at each observation point for easy relocation.

(c) Be sure to record the bearing from the observation point to each cover board location on the Cover Board form (see Illustrations 18 and 19).

(2) *Center location*

(a) An alternative method of establishing a transect is to randomly select a center point within an area to be sampled. Set angle iron or rebar at four randomly selected points 15 feet from the center point. Place the cover board at each rebar, facing the center post. Take readings and photographs of the cover board from the center point. Additional center points can be established as needed.

(b) Be sure to record the bearing and distance to each center point location from the reference post on the Cover Board form (see Illustrations 18 and 19).

e **Reference Post or Point** Permanently mark the location of each study with a reference post and a study location stake (see beginning of Section III).

f **Study Identification** Number studies for proper identification to ensure that the data collected can be positively associated with specific sites on the ground (see Appendix B).

**g  Study Documentation**  Document pertinent information concerning the study on the Study Location and Documentation Data form (see beginning of Section III and Appendix A).

7. *Taking Photographs*  The directions for establishing photo plots and for taking close-up and general view photographs are given in Section V.A.

8. *Sampling Process*  In addition to collecting the specific studies data, general observations should be made of the study sites (see Section II.F).

   Position the cover board in the appropriate locations 15 feet from the observation point.  Record the cover class from the modified Daubenmire cover classes (see Table 2) for each segment of the cover board (see Illustration 20).  Depending on the objectives, vegetative cover can be recorded by species or simply for the total of all species.  Cover can also be recorded as a straight percentage.

**Table 2**

| Cover Class | Range of Coverage | Midpoint of Range |
|:-----------:|:-----------------:|:-----------------:|
| 0 | 0% | 0% |
| T | < 1% | 0.5% |
| 1 | 1 to 5% | 3.0% |
| 2 | 5 to 25% | 15.0% |
| 3 | 25 to 50% | 37.5% |
| 4 | 50 to 75% | 62.5% |
| 5 | 75 to 95% | 85.0% |
| 6 | 95 to 100% | 97.50% |

9. *Calculations for Vertical Canopy Cover*  Calculate the average "cover score" by layer.  The midpoint of each cover class is used to calculate the average cover for each layer or for the entire transect when using cover classes.  If actual percentage estimates are made, calculate an average cover value by averaging cover for each layer.  For a total cover average, the calculation involves summing the cover values for all layers and dividing by the number of layers.

10. *Data Analysis*  For trend analysis, permanent sampling units are suggested.  If permanent transects are monitored, use the appropriate paired analysis technique.  If the transects are not permanently marked, use the appropriate nonpaired test.  When comparing more than two sampling periods, use repeated measures ANOVA.

11. *References*

Nudds, Thomas D. 1977.  Quantifying the vegetative structure of wildlife cover.  Wildlife Society Bulletin 5:113-117.

Spalinger, D.E. 1980.  Vegetation Changes on Eight Selected Deer Ranges in Nevada Over a 15-Year Period. Nevada State Office Bureau of Land Management.

USDI, Bureau of Land Management.  1987.  Riparian Inventory and Monitoring, Montana BLM Riparian Tech. Bull. No.1.

# Cover Board Method
## Density Board

| Study Number | | Date | Examiner |
|---|---|---|---|
| Allotment Name & Number | | Pasture | |

**Density Board Location -**

| | Percent Cover | | | | | | | | |
|---|---|---|---|---|---|---|---|---|---|
| | Plot 1 | | Plot 2 | | Plot 3 | | Plot 4 | | Avg. Cover |
| 5 | | | | | | | | | |
| 4 | | | | | | | | | |
| 3 | | | | | | | | | |
| 2 | | | | | | | | | |
| 1 | | | | | | | | | |

**Total Average Cover-** _____

# Cover Board Method
## Density Board

| Study Number *Duck Basin #1* | | Date *7/25/95* | Examiner *Chris Mass* |
|---|---|---|---|
| Allotment Name & Number *Duck Basin 15150* | | Pasture *Red River* | |

**Density Board Location -** *50 paces west of Countyline Road on left side of stream. Readings are taken at 48°, 139°, 228°, and 318°.*

| | Percent Cover | | | | | | | | Avg. Cover |
|---|---|---|---|---|---|---|---|---|---|
| | Plot 1 | | Plot 2 | | Plot 3 | | Plot 4 | | |
| 5 | 0 | 0 | 25 | 25 | 0 | 25 | 50 | 50 | 22 |
| 4 | 10 | 10 | 20 | 25 | 20 | 50 | 30 | 50 | 27 |
| 3 | 20 | 30 | 25 | 25 | 30 | 50 | 50 | 75 | 38 |
| 2 | 50 | 100 | 100 | 100 | 75 | 75 | 75 | 75 | 81 |
| 1 | 100 | 100 | 75 | 100 | 100 | 75 | 75 | 100 | 91 |

Total Average Cover- _____ 52 _____

Illustration 18

# Cover Board Method
## Profile Board

| Study Number | Date | Examiner | Allotment Name & Number | Pasture |
|---|---|---|---|---|
| Bearing & Distance | Study Location | | | |

### Cover Readings—Daubenmire Classes[1] or Percentages

| Observation Points | Cover Board Heights | Species | | | | | | | | | | | | Average |
|---|---|---|---|---|---|---|---|---|---|---|---|---|---|---|
| | | Bearing | | | Total | Bearing | | | Total | Bearing | | | Total | |
| | 0.0 - 0.5m | | | | | | | | | | | | | |
| | 0.5 - 1.0m | | | | | | | | | | | | | |
| | 1.0 - 1.5m | | | | | | | | | | | | | |
| | 1.5 - 2.0m | | | | | | | | | | | | | |
| | 0.0 - 0.5m | | | | | | | | | | | | | |
| | 0.5 - 1.0m | | | | | | | | | | | | | |
| | 1.0 - 1.5m | | | | | | | | | | | | | |
| | 1.5 - 2.0m | | | | | | | | | | | | | |
| | 0.0 - 0.5m | | | | | | | | | | | | | |
| | 0.5 - 1.0m | | | | | | | | | | | | | |
| | 1.0 - 1.5m | | | | | | | | | | | | | |
| | 1.5 - 2.0m | | | | | | | | | | | | | |
| | 0.0 - 0.5m | | | | | | | | | | | | | |
| | 0.5 - 1.0m | | | | | | | | | | | | | |
| | 1.0 - 1.5m | | | | | | | | | | | | | |
| | 1.5 - 2.0m | | | | | | | | | | | | | |

Comments:

[1] Daubenmire Classes: 0=0; 1=1-5; 2=5-25; 3=25-50; 4=50-75; 5=75-95; 6=95-100

Illustration 19

91

# Cover Board Method
## Profile Board

| Study Number | Date | Examiner | Allotment Name & Number | Pasture |
|---|---|---|---|---|
| Mule Creek #2 | 7/12/95 | Joe Lewis | Mule Creek – 16171 | River |

**Bearing & Distance:** 15° – 25 paces

**Study Location:** 1/8 mile upstream from Baker Road. EAST Side of stream.

Cover Readings—Daubenmire Classes[1] or Percentages

Species

| Obs. Points | Cover Board Heights | Bearing | CAREY POA | SABI | ALNUS | Total | Bearing | CAREY POA | SABI | ALNUS | Total | Bearing | CAREY POA | SABI | ALNUS | Total | Bearing | CAREY | SABI | ALNUS | Total | Average |
|---|---|---|---|---|---|---|---|---|---|---|---|---|---|---|---|---|---|---|---|---|---|---|
| 1 | 0.0 - 0.5m | 151° | 20 | 56 | 21 | 97 | 241° | 4 | 38 | 12 | 54 | 331° | 33 | 1 | 62 | 96 | 61° | 21 | 6 | 33 | 60 | 77 |
|   | 0.5 - 1.0m |  | 0 | 48 | 18 | 66 |  | 0 | 31 | 8 | 39 |  | 0 | 18 | 75 | 93 |  | 0 | 28 | 41 | 69 | 67 |
|   | 1.0 - 1.5m |  | 0 | 30 | 15 | 45 |  | 0 | 26 | 3 | 29 |  | 0 | 0 | 98 | 98 |  | 0 | 18 | 25 | 43 | 54 |
|   | 1.5 - 2.0m |  | 0 | 25 | 10 | 35 |  | 0 | 12 | 1 | 13 |  | 0 | 0 | 98 | 98 |  | 0 | 10 | 18 | 28 | 44 |
| 2 | 0.0 - 0.5m | 230° | 15 | 31 | 38 | 84 | 320° | 30 | 14 | 31 | 75 | 50° | 21 | 44 | 30 | 95 | 140° | 28 | 6 | 50 | 84 | 85 |
|   | 0.5 - 1.0m |  | 0 | 50 | 15 | 65 |  | 0 | 38 | 37 | 75 |  | 0 | 53 | 40 | 93 |  | 0 | 51 | 24 | 75 | 77 |
|   | 1.0 - 1.5m |  | 0 | 59 | 19 | 78 |  | 0 | 57 | 20 | 71 |  | 0 | 59 | 33 | 92 |  | 0 | 59 | 16 | 75 | 79 |
|   | 1.5 - 2.0m |  | 0 | 31 | 52 | 83 |  | 0 | 52 | 34 | 86 |  | 0 | 49 | 26 | 75 |  | 0 | 37 | 46 | 83 | 82 |
| 3 | 0.0 - 0.5m | 66° | 18 | 17 | 22 | 57 | 156° | 1 | 25 | 52 | 78 | 246° | 6 | 45 | 36 | 87 | 336° | 9 | 20 | 41 | 70 | 73 |
|   | 0.5 - 1.0m |  | 0 | 54 | 19 | 73 |  | 0 | 56 | 35 | 91 |  | 0 | 13 | 40 | 53 |  | 0 | 45 | 37 | 82 | 75 |
|   | 1.0 - 1.5m |  | 0 | 48 | 27 | 75 |  | 0 | 33 | 24 | 57 |  | 0 | 16 | 38 | 54 |  | 0 | 55 | 45 | 99 | 71 |
|   | 1.5 - 2.0m |  | 0 | 52 | 35 | 87 |  | 0 | 46 | 24 | 70 |  | 0 | 21 | 51 | 72 |  | 0 | 44 | 28 | 72 | 75 |
| 4 | 0.0 - 0.5m | 358° | 12 | 21 | 47 | 80 | 88° | 6 | 14 | 57 | 77 | 178° | 12 | 39 | 20 | 71 | 268° | 13 | 41 | 39 | 92 | 80 |
|   | 0.5 - 1.0m |  | 0 | 18 | 46 | 64 |  | 0 | 10 | 54 | 64 |  | 0 | 28 | 61 | 89 |  | 0 | 29 | 31 | 60 | 69 |
|   | 1.0 - 1.5m |  | 0 | 54 | 39 | 93 |  | 0 | 53 | 0 | 53 |  | 0 | 55 | 36 | 91 |  | 0 | 54 | 24 | 79 | 79 |
|   | 1.5 - 2.0m |  | 0 | 28 | 45 | 73 |  | 0 | 0 | 0 | 0 |  | 0 | 26 | 0 | 26 |  | 0 | 23 | 28 | 51 | 59 |

**Comments:** Percentages used.

[1] Daubenmire Classes: 0=0; 1=1-5; 2=5-25; 3=25-50; 4=50-75; 5=75-95; 6=95-100

**Illustration 19**

## Examples of Cover Boards

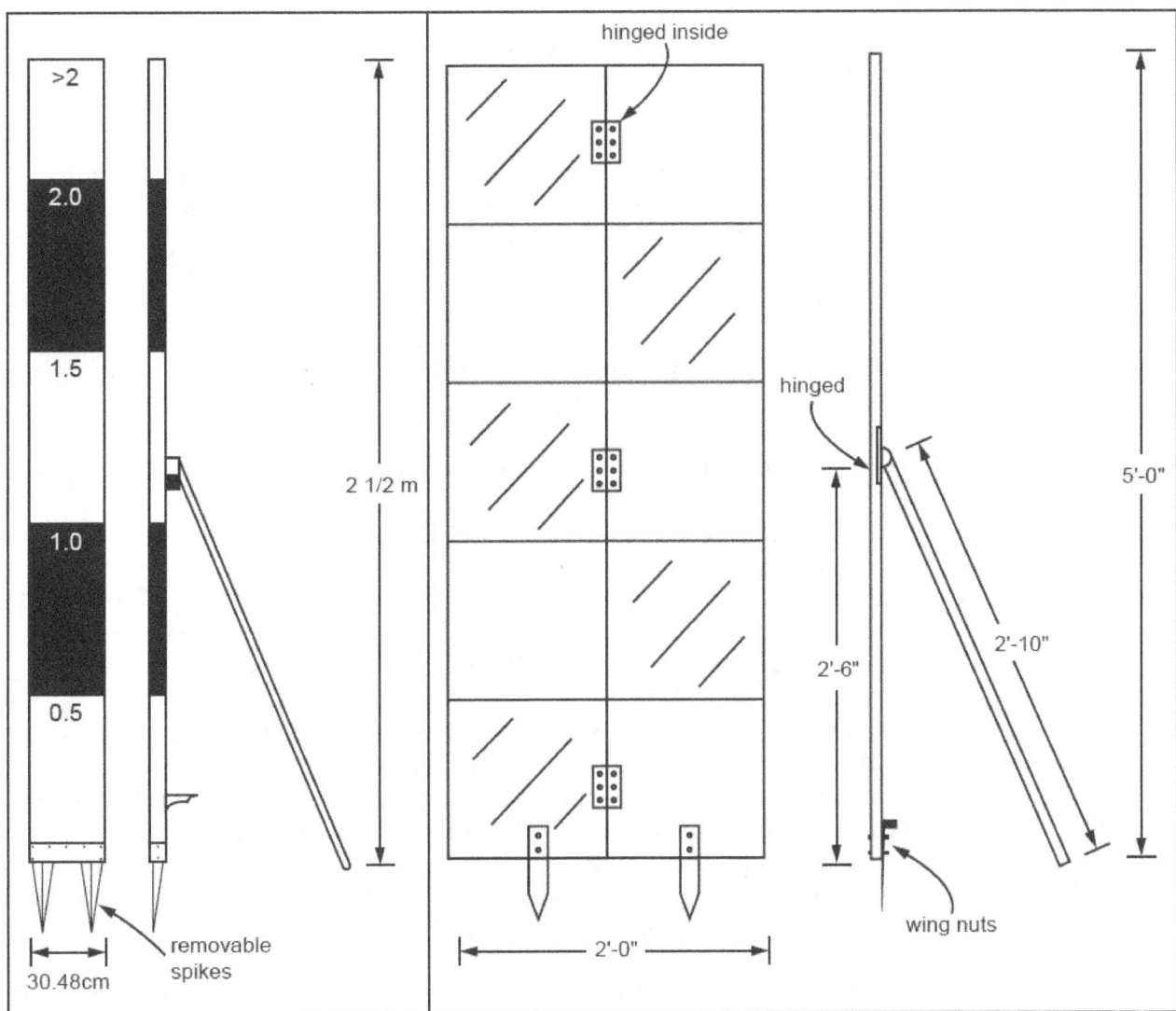

**Profile Board**

**Density Board**

Illustration 20

93

# I. Density Method

1. *General Description* Density is the number of individuals of a species in a given unit of area. For rhizomatous and other species for which the delineation of separate individual plants is difficult, density can also mean the number of stems, inflorescences, culm groups, or other plant parts per unit area.

2. *Areas of Use* This method has wide applicability and is suited for use with grasses, forbs, shrubs, and trees.

3. *Advantages and Limitations*

   a Generally, the density of mature perennial plants is not affected as much by annual variations in precipitation as are other vegetation attributes such as canopy cover or herbage production.

   b Density is a quantifiable and absolute attribute.

   c Density is sensitive to changes in the adult population caused by long-term climatic conditions or resource uses.

   d Density provides useful information on seedling emergence, survival, and mortality.

   e Sampling is often quick and easy with certain life forms (e.g., trees, shrubs, bunchgrasses).

   f Plant communities on the same ecological sites can be compared using density estimates on specific species or lifeforms.

   g Density can be useful in estimating plant responses to management actions.

   h It can often be difficult to delineate an individual, especially when sampling sod forming plants (stoloniferous, or rhizomatous plants) and multi-stemmed grasses or closely spaced shrubs. Although in these cases a surrogate plant part (e.g., upright stems, inflorescences, culm groups) can be counted, the usefulness of such estimates is limited to the biological significance of changes in these surrogates.

   i Sampling may be slow and tedious in dense populations; this also raises the risk of non-sampling errors.

   j There is no single quadrat size and shape that will efficiently and adequately sample all species and life forms. For this reason, density estimations are usually limited to one or a few key species.

4. *Equipment* The following equipment is needed (see also the equipment listed in Section V.A, page 31, for the establishment of the photo plot):

   - Study Location and Documentation Data form (see Appendix A)
   - Density form (see Illustration 21)
   - Tapes: 50-, 100-, 150-, or 200-meter delineated in centimeters. (Tapes in

English measurements can be substituted but metric tapes are preferred.) At least three tapes are required (one, to be used for constructing quadrats, need only be as long as the long side of the quadrat; a rope of the desired length can be substituted for this tape); four are better.

- Meter sticks (or yard sticks if using English measurements). Two are required.
- Four stakes: 3/4- or 1-inch angle iron not less than 16 inches long
- Hammer
- Permanent yellow or orange spray paint
- Tally counter (optional)
- Compass
- Steel post and driver

5. *Training* As with any monitoring method, adequate training is essential to minimize nonsampling errors.

   **a** Examiners must be able to identify the target plant species.

   **b** For sod-forming grasses and other species for which individual plants might be hard to distinguish, written guidelines should be provided on what constitutes an individual unit to be counted.[6] This will help to ensure consistency among examiners. To assess consistency prior to the study, several examiners should be asked to independently count these units in the same set of quadrats and the results compared. If relatively consistent results cannot be achieved a different species should be chosen for estimation or a different method selected.

6. *Establishing Studies* Careful establishment of studies is a critical element in obtaining meaningful data.

   **a Site Selection** The most important factor in obtaining usable data is selecting representative areas (critical or key areas) in which to run the study (see Section II.D). Study sites should be located within a single plant community within a single ecological site. Transects and sampling points need to be randomly located within the critical or key areas (see Section III).

   **b Pilot Studies** Collect data on several pilot studies to determine the number of samples (transects or observation points) and the number and size of quadrats needed to collect a statistically valid sample (see Section III.B.8).

   (1) *Quadrat size and shape* It is vital to choose the quadrat size and shape that will give the highest statistical precision for the area and key species being sampled. As a general rule of thumb long, thin quadrats are better

---

[6] Determination of what constitutes a unit to be counted is somewhat arbitrary. For rhizomatous grasses such as western wheatgrass (*Pascopyrum smithii*), each culm group can be visualized as an actual or potential plant unit, as can rooted stoloniferous units of such species as vine mesquite (*Panicum obtusum*). Mat or sod-forming plants such as blue grama (*Bouteloua gracilis*) or alkali sacaton (*Sporobolus airoides*) usually start growth as small, distinct clumps, but may spread to plants a meter or more in diameter. As this occurs they tend to fragment into more-or-less separate units, and it is these separate units that should be counted as actual or potential individuals. For rhizomatous or mat-forming forbs, flowering stems may be the units counted. The examiner should ensure, however, that a change in the unit chosen is of biological significance, i.e., reflects a real change in the vegetation community. If it has no such significance, then another unit or a different species should be chosen. (Alternatively, an attribute other than density can be selected for monitoring.)

(often very much better) than circles, squares, or shorter and wider quadrats (Krebs 1989). How narrow the quadrats can be depends upon consideration of measurement errors due to edge effect, but these problems can be largely overcome by incorporating rules for determining whether a plant falls inside or outside a quadrat (discussed in more detail under Sampling Process below).

(a) Subjectively place quadrats[7] of a certain size and shape in areas with large numbers of the target plant species. See how many plants fall into the quadrat and ask if this is too many to count. See what kind of problems there might be with edge effect: when individuals fall on or near one of the long edges of the quadrat, will it be difficult for examiners to make consistent calls as to whether these individuals are in or out of the quadrat? See if there is a tendency to get more plants in rectangular quadrats when they are run one way as opposed to another.

(b) Determine the standard deviations of those quadrat sizes and shapes deemed to be practical from the subjective examination described above (see Section III.B.8.b).

(c) Choose the quadrat size and shape with the smallest standard deviation.

(2) ***Direction of quadrats*** Determine if there is an environmental gradient affecting the density of the target species in the key area. Examples of such gradients are elevation and moisture. If there is a gradient, the study should be set up so that the long side of each quadrat is placed *perpendicular* to this gradient. This ensures that there is more variability *within* each quadrat than there is *between* quadrats.

Subjectively placing quadrats in different directions as described under 6.b.(1)(a) above can assist in making this determination. For example, if quadrats laid out with the long side going north-south tend to have no or fewer plants of the key species than quadrats with the long side going east-west, the east-west position should be selected.

c **Study Layout** Data can be collected using the baseline, macroplot or linear study designs described in Section III.A.2 beginning on page 8. The macroplot technique is the recommended procedure.

d **Reference Post or Point** Permanently mark the location of each study with a reference post and a study location stake (see beginning of Section III).

e **Study Identification** Number macroplots for proper identification to ensure

---

[7] Note that it is not necessary to construct an actual frame for the quadrats used. It is sufficient to delineate quadrats using a combination of tape measures and meter (or yard) sticks. For example, a 5 m x 0.25 m quadrat can be constructed by selecting a 5 m interval along a meter tape, placing two 1-meter sticks perpendicular to the tape at both ends of the interval (with their zero points at the tape), and laying another tape or rope across these two sticks at their 0.25 m points. This then circumscribes a quadrat of the desired size and shape. Alternately place a meter stick perpendicular to the tape at one end of the interval. The meter stick is then moved slowly up the interval and all plants of the species occurring within the first 0.25 m of the meter stick recorded until the end of the interval is reached.

that the data collected can be positively associated with specific sites on the ground (see Appendix B).

f **Study Documentation** Document pertinent information concerning the study on the Study Location and Documentation Data form (see beginning of Section III and Appendix A).

7. *Taking Photographs* The directions for establishing photo plots and for taking close-up and general view photographs are given in Section V.A.

8. *Sampling Process* In addition to collecting the specific studies data, general observations should be made of the study sites (see Section II.F).

a **Selecting Random Pairs of Coordinates** Using the technique described in Section III.A.2.b.(2) on page 10 and Appendix D, select coordinates to mark the points at which quadrats will be positioned.

b **Sampling** Assuming that the x-axis is on the "bottom" and the y-axis is at the "left," each pair of coordinates represents the lower left corner of each quadrat. Thus, if one random set of coordinates is 0,0, the quadrat is positioned with its lower left corner at the origin.

(1) Place the quadrats at each of the random pairs of coordinates and continue reading them until the number of quadrats previously determined to be required has been read.

Make a quadrat of the desired size and shape by running a tape in the direction of the long side of each quadrat from the appropriate axis and using two 1-meter sticks and another tape or rope. In the example in Section III.A.2.b.(2)(e) on page 11, it has been decided that the quadrats should be placed with their long sides parallel to the x-axis and that the quadrats should be 1 m x 16 m. Based on the random coordinates chosen, the first quadrat is to be placed at the 28 m point on the y-axis and the 16 m point on the x-axis. A tape is run parallel to the x-axis beginning at the 28 m point on the y-axis. At the 16 m mark on this tape, a meter stick is positioned perpendicular to the tape with its 0 point at the tape. Another meter stick is similarly placed at the 32 m mark. Another tape or a rope of 16 m in length is placed across the two 1-meter sticks at their 1 m points. The number of plants is counted in this quadrat and sampling continues. If the short side of each quadrat exceeds 1.0 m, more than one 1-meter stick or additional tapes or ropes may need to be used.

(2) Count the number of individuals (or other counting unit) of the key species in each quadrat and record this on the Density form (Illustration 21). Count only those plants that are rooted in the quadrat. Often it is desir-

able to make separate counts for different size or age classes of the key species. This is particularly true for seedlings, many of which may not survive to the next sampling period.

(a) To eliminate measurement error due to edge effects, it is helpful to have rules for determining whether an individual plant that falls exactly on the edge of a quadrat is considered inside or outside the quadrat.

(b) A good rule to follow is to count those individuals falling on the left and top edges of the quadrat as being inside the quadrat and those individuals falling on the right and bottom edges of the quadrat as being outside the quadrat. Make sure that all observers follow the same set of rules.

9. *Calculations* Make the calculations and record the results on the Density form (see Illustration 21).

   a **Average Density per Quadrat** Calculate the estimated average density per quadrat for each size/age class by dividing the total number of plants counted in the sample for each size/age class by the number of quadrats in the sample. If more than one key species is counted, this process is done separately for each species. For example, a sample of 40 quadrats yields a total of 177 individual mature plants of key species Y. The estimated average density of mature plants per quadrat is therefore 177/40 = 4.4 plants/quadrat.

   b **Total Density of Macroplot** Calculate the estimated total density of the macroplot by multiplying the average density per quadrat by the total number of possible quadrats in the macroplot. If more than one key species is counted, this process is done separately for each key species. Say the macroplot in the example given in 9.a above is 40 m x 80 m and the quadrat size is 1.0 m x 16 m. There are 200 possible nonoverlapping quadrat placements in a macroplot of this size (40/1 = 40 along one axis and 80/16 = 5 along the other; 40 x 5 = 200 possible quadrats). The estimate of the total density of the macroplot is there-fore 4.4 mature plants/quadrat x 200 quadrats = 880 mature plants.

10. *Data Analysis and Interpretation* Data analysis is straightforward. Confidence intervals should be constructed around each of the estimates of average density per quadrat (hereafter referred to simply as "average") and total macroplot density for each year. The averages of two years should be compared by using a *t* test (for independent samples). Averages of three or more years can be compared by an analysis of variance. See Technical Reference, *Measuring & Monitoring Plant Populations*.

11. *References*

Krebs, C.J. 1989. Ecological methodology. Harper & Row, New York. This book discusses the superiority of long, thin quadrats over circular and square quadrats, as well as the potential problems of edge effect.

Salzer, D. 1994.  An introduction to sampling and sampling design for vegetation monitoring. Unpublished papers prepared for Bureau of Land Management Training Course 1730-5. BLM Training Center, Phoenix, Arizona. These papers, together with material prepared for a class exercise, present the basic concepts of the Density Method.  The Density Method is in rather widespread use in The Nature Conservancy and, increasingly, by the Bureau of Land Management and the Forest Service, particularly as a means of estimating numbers of special status plant species.

# Density

| Study Number | Date | Examiner | Allotment Name & Number | | | | | | | | | Pasture | | Plot Size |
|---|---|---|---|---|---|---|---|---|---|---|---|---|---|---|
| Study Location | | | | | | | | | | | | | | |

| Plot | 1 | | 2 | | 3 | | 4 | | 5 | | 6 | | 7 | | 8 | | 9 | | 10 | | Total | |
|---|---|---|---|---|---|---|---|---|---|---|---|---|---|---|---|---|---|---|---|---|---|---|
| Coordinates | | | | | | | | | | | | | | | | | | | | | | |
| Plant Species | Mature | Seedling | Mature | Seedling | Mature | Seedling | Mature | Seedling | Mature | Seedling | Mature | Seedling | Mature | Seedling | Mature | Seedling | Mature | Seedling | Mature | Seedling | Mature | Seedling |

Illustration 21

# Density

| Study Number | Date | Examiner | Allotment Name & Number | Pasture | Plot Size |
|---|---|---|---|---|---|
| Empire #4 | 9/6/96 | Cindy Cone | Empire - 21206 | South | 16 m² |

Study Location: Study is 2 mi. south of Antelope fence on the EAST side of the road.

| Plot | 1 | | 2 | | 3 | | 4 | | 5 | | 6 | | 7 | | 8 | | 9 | | 10 | | Total | |
|---|---|---|---|---|---|---|---|---|---|---|---|---|---|---|---|---|---|---|---|---|---|---|
| Coordinates | 0 | 3 | 0 | 4 | 16 | 7 | 16 | 48 | 32 | 21 | 32 | 27 | 32 | 38 | 48 | 8 | 48 | 27 | 64 | 34 | | |
| Plant Species | Mature | Seedling | Mature | Seedling | Mature | Seedling | Mature | Seedling | Mature | Seedling | Mature | Seedling | Mature | Seedling | Mature | Seedling | Mature | Seedling | Mature | Seedling | Mature | Seedling |
| HIBE | 6 | 3 | 5 | 2 | 6 | 3 | | | 6 | 6 | 11 | 6 | | | 7 | | | | | 6 | 41 | 23 |
| BOHI | 4 | | | | 3 | | | | | | | | 10 | | 4 | | | | | | 21 | |
| BOER 4 | 1 | | | | | | | | | 3 | | | 1 | | | | | | | | 5 | |
| HATE | 3 | | | | | | 3 | | | | | | | | | | 4 | 1 | | | 10 | 1 |
| LYPH | 10 | | 4 | | | | 2 | 6 | | | | | 4 | | | | | | | | 20 | 6 |
| AAFF | 3 | | | | 1 | | | | | | | | | | | | | | | 8 | 4 | 8 |
| Lupine | | | | | | | | | | | | | | | 4 | | 2 | | | 5 | 6 | 5 |
| BOCU | | | | | | | | | | | | | | | 1 | | | | | | 1 | |
| BOGR | | | | | | | | | | | | | | | | | 13 | | | | 13 | |

Illustration 21    101

# J. Double-Weight Sampling

1. *General Description* This technique has been referred to by some as the Calibrated Weight Estimate method. The objective of this method is to determine the amount of current-year above-ground vegetation production on a defined area. The following vegetation attributes are monitored:

   - Peak standing crop, which is the above-ground annual production of each plant species

   - Species composition by weight

   It is important to establish a photo plot (see Section V.A) and take both close-up and general view photographs. This allows the portrayal of resource values and conditions and furnishes visual evidence of vegetation and soil changes over time.

2. *Areas of Use* This method can be used in a wide variety of vegetation types. It is best suited to grasslands and desert shrubs. It can also be used in large shrub and tree communities, but the difficulties increase.

3. *Advantages and Limitations*

   a Double-weight sampling measures the attribute historically used to determine capabilities of an ecosystem.

   b It provides the basic data currently used for determining ecological status.

   c Seasonal and annual fluctuations in climate can influence plant biomass.

   d Measurements can be time-consuming.

   e Current year's growth can be hard to separate from previous years' growth.

   f Accurate measurements require collecting production data at peak production periods, which are usually short, or using utilization and phenology adjustment factors.

   g Green weights require conversion to air-dry weights.

   h In most areas, the variability in production between quadrats and the accuracy of estimating production within individual quadrats requires the sampling of large numbers of quadrats in order to detect reasonable levels of change.

4. *Equipment* The following equipment is needed (see also the equipment listed in Section V.A, page 31, for the establishment of the photo plot):

   - Study Location and Documentation Data form (see Appendix A)
   - Production form (Illustration 22)
   - Sampling frames or hoops
   - One stake: 3/4- or 1-inch angle iron not less than 16 inches long

- Herbage Yield Tables for Trees by Height, DBH, or Canopy
- Clippers
- Paper bags
- Kilogram and gram spring-loaded scales with clip
- Tree diameter measuring tape
- Steel post & driver
- Oven for drying vegetation
- Air-dry weight conversion tables
- Rubber bands
- Pin flags
- Compass

5. *Training* The accuracy of the data depends on the training and ability of the examiners. Examiners must be able to identify plant species and determine current year's growth.

6. *Establishing Studies* Careful establishment of studies is a critical element in obtaining meaningful data (see Section III).

   a **Site Selection** The most important factor in obtaining usable data is selecting representative areas (critical or key areas) in which to run the study (see Section II.D). Study sites should be located within a single plant community within a single ecological site. Transects and sampling points need to be randomly located within the critical or key areas (see Section III).

      (1) The number of quadrats selected depends on the purpose for which the estimates are to be used, uniformity of the vegetation, and other factors (see Section III.B for Statistical Considerations).

      (2) The size and shape of quadrats must be adapted to the vegetation community to be sampled (see Section III.B.6).

   b **Pilot Studies** Collect data on several pilot studies to determine the number of samples (transects or observation points) and the number and size of quadrats needed to collect a statistically valid sample (see Section III.B.8).

   c **Study Layout** Production data can be collected using either the baseline, macroplot or linear study designs described in Section III.A.2 beginning on page 8. The linear technique is the one most often used.

   d **Number of Transects** Establish the minimum number of transects to achieve the desired level of precision for the key species in each study site (see Section III.B).

   e **Reference Post or Point** Permanently mark the location of each study with a reference post and a study location stake (see beginning of Section III).

   f **Study Identification** Number studies for proper identification to ensure that the data collected can be positively associated with specific sites on the ground (see Appendix B).

**g Study and Documentation** Document pertinent information concerning the study on the Study Location and Documentation Data form (see beginning of Section III and Appendix A).

7. *Taking Photographs* The directions for establishing photo plots and for taking close-up and general view photographs are given in Section V.A.

8. *Weight Units* Double sampling requires the establishment of a weight unit for each species occurring in the area to be sampled. All weight units are based on current year's growth.

**a Procedures For Establishing Weight Units:**

(1) Decide on a weight unit that is appropriate for each species. A weight unit could be an entire plant, a group of plants, or an easily identifiable portion of a plant, and can be measured in either pounds or grams.

(2) Visually select a representative weight unit.

(3) Harvest and weigh the plant material to determine the actual weight of the weight unit.

(4) Maintain proficiency in estimating by periodically harvesting and weighing to check estimates of production.

**b Estimating Production of a Single Quadrat:**

(1) Estimate production by counting the weight units of each species in the quadrat.

(2) Convert weight units for each species to grams or pounds.

(3) Harvest and weigh each species to check estimate of production.

(4) Repeat the process until proficiency is attained.

(5) Periodically repeat the process to maintain proficiency in estimating.

(6) Keep the harvested material, when necessary, for air-drying and weighing to convert from green weights to air-dry weights.

**c Alternate Method of Establishing Weight Units:**

(1) Decide on a weight unit that is appropriate for each species. A weight unit could be an entire plant, a group of plants, or an easily identifiable portion of a plant, and can be measured in either pounds or grams.

(2) Visually select a representative weight unit.

(3) Instead of weighing the material, save it by securing it with rubber bands so portions are not lost.

(4) Use this as a visual model for comparison at each quadrat in the transect. Record on the proper forms only the number of weight units. Do not record the estimated weights.

(5) Weigh each weight unit at the conclusion of the transect. Weighing the weight unit before the conclusion of the transect might influence the weight estimates.

(6) Convert the weight units on the form to actual weight by multiplying the number of units by the weight of the unit.

(7) Harvested weight unit material is *not* saved for determining air-dry weight conversion. Air-dry conversions are determined from clipped quadrats.

9. *Sampling Process* In addition to collecting the specific studies data, general observations should be made of the study sites (see Section II.F).

   a **Transect Bearing** Determine the transect bearing and select a prominent distant landmark such as a peak, rocky point, etc., that can be used as the transect bearing point.

   b **Double Sampling**

   (1) Randomly select the starting point along the transect bearing. Take the specified number of paces and read the first quadrat.

   (2) Temporarily mark the quadrat by placing a pin flag next to the quadrat so that it can be relocated later if this quadrat is selected for clipping. Be sure to flag every quadrat.

   (3) Estimate and record the weight of each species in the quadrat by means of the weight-unit method.

   When estimating or harvesting plants, include all parts of all plants *within* the quadrat. Exclude *all* parts of herbaceous plants and shrubs outside the vertical projection of the quadrat, even though the base is within the quadrat (see Illustration 23).

   (4) Continue the transect by establishing additional quadrats at specified pace intervals. To change the length of the transect, adjust the number of paces between quadrats.

   (5) After weights have been estimated on all quadrats, select the quadrats to be harvested.

   (a) The quadrats selected should include all or most of the species in the estimated quadrats. If an important species occurs on some of the estimated quadrats but not on the harvested quadrats, it can be clipped *individually* on one or more other quadrats.

(b) The number of quadrats harvested depends on the number estimated. At least one quadrat should be harvested for each seven estimated to adequately correct the estimates (see table 3).

Table 3

| Number of quadrats Estimated | Minimum Number of Quadrats to be Weighed |
|---|---|
| 1 - 7 | 1 |
| 8 - 14 | 2 |
| 14 - 21 | 3 |
| 22 - 28 | 4 |
| 29 - 35 | 5 |
| 36 - 42 | 6 |

(6) Harvest, weigh, and record the weight of each species in the quadrats selected for harvesting. Harvest all herbaceous plants originating in the quadrat at ground level. On rangeland, harvest *all* of the current leaf, twig, and fruit production of woody plants located in the quadrats. On native pasture and grazable woodland, harvest the current leaf, twig, and fruit production of woody plants within the plot up to a height of 4 1/2 feet above the ground. For further clarification see Illustration 23.

(7) Correct estimated weights by dividing the harvested weight of *each species* by the estimated weight for the corresponding species on the harvested quadrats. This factor is used to correct the estimates for that species in each quadrat. A factor of more than 1.0 indicates that the estimate is too low. A factor lower than 1.0 indicates that the estimate is too high.

After quadrats are estimated and harvested and correction factors for estimates are computed, air-dry percentages are determined by air-drying the harvested materials or by selecting the appropriate factor from an air-dry percentage table. Values for each species are then converted to air-dry pound per acre or kilograms per hectare for all quadrats. Average weight and percentage composition can then be computed for the sample area.

10. *Calculations* The weights collected for each species per quadrat placement are recorded on the Production form (see Illustration 22).

a Record estimated weights for each species occurring in each quadrat in the appropriate column (Estimated or Clipped Weight sections of the form.)

b Quadrats that were harvested are circled. The estimate weights for these quadrats are totaled and shown in column 4. The total harvested weights are shown in column 5. Harvested weights for each quadrat for each species are not shown on the form, only the total for each species.

c Column 6 is the actual dry weight for each species from the quadrats that were clipped.

**d** The Quadrat Correction Factor (QCF)column 7 is calculated by dividing column 5 by column 4.

**f** Column 8 is determined by dividing the dry weight by the green weight. In the example shown on Illustration 22, the clipped weights were not air dried; the percent dry weights shown in column 8 were taken from the dry weight conversion table.

**g** The total estimated weights for each species for the entire transect are shown in column 9.

**h** The average yield (column 10) is determined by multiplying the Total Estimated Weight of each species (column 9) times the Quadrat Correction Factor (column 7) to adjust for the error in estimating weights and then multiplying that times the percent dry weight (column 8) to determine the adjusted dry weight or the Average Yield (column 10).

**i** The Average Yield for each species (column 10) is totaled at the bottom of the form for the composition totals.

**j** Percent Composition (column 11) is calculated by dividing the average yield for each species (column 10) by the composition totals.

**k** If peak standing crop is collected in grams, it can be easily converted to pounds per acres if the total area sampled is a multiple of 9.6 ft$^2$.

Use table 4 to convert grams to pounds per acre:

### Table 4

(# of plots x size = total area)

| | | | | |
|---|---|---|---|---|
| (10 x 0.96 | = | 9.6 ft$^2$) | multiply grams times 10.0 | = pounds per acre |
| (10 x 1.92 | = | 19.2 ft$^2$) | multiply grams times 5.0 | = pounds per acre |
| (10 x 2.40 | = | 24.0 ft$^2$) | multiply grams times 4.0 | = pounds per acre |
| (10 x 4.80 | = | 48.0 ft$^2$) | multiply grams times 2.0 | = pounds per acre |
| (10 x 9.60 | = | 96.0 ft$^2$) | multiply grams times 1.0 | = pounds per acre |
| (10 x 96.0 | = | 960.0 ft$^2$) | multiply grams times 0.1 | = pounds per acre |

11. *Data Analysis* This technique involves destructive sampling (clipped plots), so permanent transects or quadrats are not recommended. Since the transects are not permanently marked, use the appropriate nonpaired test. When comparing more than two sampling periods, use ANOVA.

12. *References*

Cook, C. Wayne and James Stubbendieck, 1986. Range Research: Basic Problems and Techniques. Society for Range Management. Denver, CO.

Laycock, W.A. 1987. Setting Objectives and Picking Appropriate Methods for Monitoring Vegetation on Rangelands. Rangeland Monitoring Workshop Proceedings. U.S. Department of Interior. Bureau of Land Management. Golden, CO.

Pechanec, J.F. and G.D. Pickford. 1937. A weight-estimate method for the determination of range or pasture production. J. Amer. Soc. Agron. 29:894-904.

Riser, Paul G. 1984. Methods for Inventory and Monitoring of Vegetation, Litter, and Soil Surface Condition. Developing Strategies for Rangeland Monitoring. National Research Council National Academy of Sciences.

USDA, Soil Conservation Service. 1976. National Range Handbook. 154 p.

USDI, Bureau of Land Management. 1984 (rev. 1990). National Range Handbook 4410-1. Washington, D. C.

Van Dyne, George M., W.G. Vogel, and H.G. Fisser. 1963. Influence of small plot size and shape on range herbage production estimates. Ecology 44:746-759.

# Production

| | | | | Study Number | | Date | | Examiner | | Allotment Name & Number | | | Pasture | |
|---|---|---|---|---|---|---|---|---|---|---|---|---|---|---|

| Transect Location | | | | | | | | | | Quadrat Size | | Transect Bearing | | |

| Plant | Estimated or Clipped Weight Per Species | | | | | | | | | | Wt Clipped Plots | | | %Dry | Wt All | Avg | Pct |
|---|---|---|---|---|---|---|---|---|---|---|---|---|---|---|---|---|---|
| Symbol | (Circle Plots that are Clipped) (3) | | | | | | | | | | Est | Clip | Dry | QCF | Wt | Plots | Yield | Comp |
| Plant Name | P-1 | P-2 | P-3 | P-4 | P-5 | P-6 | P-7 | P-8 | P-9 | P-10 | | | | | | | | |
| (2) | | | | | | | | | | | (4) | (5) | (6) | (7) | (8) | (9) | (10) | (11) |
| (1) | | | | | | | | | | | | | | | | | | |

Totals

Notes (use other side or another page)

Illustration 22

# Production

| Study Number 13N-41E-27-04 | Date 9/30/95 | Examiner Rex Johnson | Allotment Name & Number Round Mtn 11078 | Pasture Ridge |
|---|---|---|---|---|

Transect Location: 2 miles north of Jack's well on the left hand side of the road.

Quadrat Size 96 sq. ft.  
Transect Bearing 225°

| Plant Name (1) | Symbol (2) | P-1 | P-2 | P-3 | P-4 | P-5 | P-6 | P-7 | P-8 | P-9 | P-10 | Est (4) | Clip (5) | Dry (6) | QCF (7) | %Dry Wt (8) | Wt All Plots (9) | Avg Yield (10) | Pct Comp (11) |
|---|---|---|---|---|---|---|---|---|---|---|---|---|---|---|---|---|---|---|---|
| Black Grama | BOER2 | 12 | 16 | ⑤ | 16 | | 8 | | 3 | 8 | 3 | 8 | 9 | | 1.12 | 55 | 71 | 43.7 | 12 |
| Curly Mesquite | HIbe | 7 | 12 | 12 | 7 | | 4 | 9 | | 3 | 3 | 12 | 13 | | 1.08 | 60 | 42 | 27.2 | 8 |
| Blue Grama | BOGR2 | 3 | 4 | 3 | 7 | 4 | | 1 | 8 | | 5 | 8 | 7 | | .87 | 60 | 35 | 18.3 | 5 |
| Sideoats Grama | BOCU | | 8 | 1 | | | 12 | 5 | | 7 | 3 | 3 | 4 | | 1.33 | 55 | 36 | 26.3 | 7 |
| Bush Muhly | MUPO2 | | | | | ③ | | | | | | 3 | 3 | | 1.00 | 55 | 3 | 1.6 | 1 |
| Sixweeks Grama | BOBA | | | 1 | | | | | 6 | 2 | 6 | 7 | 8 | | 1.14 | 60 | 15 | 10.3 | 3 |
| 3-AWN | ARIST | | | 10 | | | | 5 | | | 8 | 18 | 16 | | .88 | 60 | 23 | 12.1 | 3 |
| | VUOC | | | | | 3 | 1 | | | 3 | 3 | 3 | 2 | | .66 | 55 | 10 | 3.6 | 1 |
| | Gilia | 3 | | 5 | 8 | 5 | 1 | 1 | 2 | 12 | 1 | 6 | 7 | | 1.16 | 40 | 32 | 14.8 | 4 |
| Lotus | | 2 | 1 | | 3 | 5 | | 1 | 5 | 6 | 6 | 6 | 7 | | 1.16 | 40 | 23 | 10.7 | 3 |
| Lupin | | | 3 | 2 | | 6 | 1 | 7 | 2 | 2 | 1 | 3 | 4 | | 1.33 | 40 | 22 | 11.7 | 3 |
| Pepperweed | | | | | 2 | | 2 | | 3 | 4 | 3 | 3 | 4 | | 1.33 | 40 | 14 | 7.4 | 2 |
| Burroweed | HAGR | 25 | | 18 | 12 | | 30 | | | 7 | | 18 | 20 | | 1.11 | 65 | 92 | 66.4 | 18 |
| Mesquite | PRJU | | 32 | 20 | | 20 | 45 | | 15 | 28 | | 28 | 31 | | 1.10 | 50 | 140 | 77 | 21 |
| Wolfberry | Lyph | | | 20 | | | | 12 | | 15 | | 20 | 22 | | 1.10 | 65 | 47 | 33.6 | 9 |
| Totals | | | | | | | | | | | | | | | | | 364.7 | | 100 |

Notes (use other side or another page)

110

Illustration 22

# Weight Estimate Quadrat

Record weights of all plants within the vertical projection of the quadrat even though the base is *not* within the quadrat.

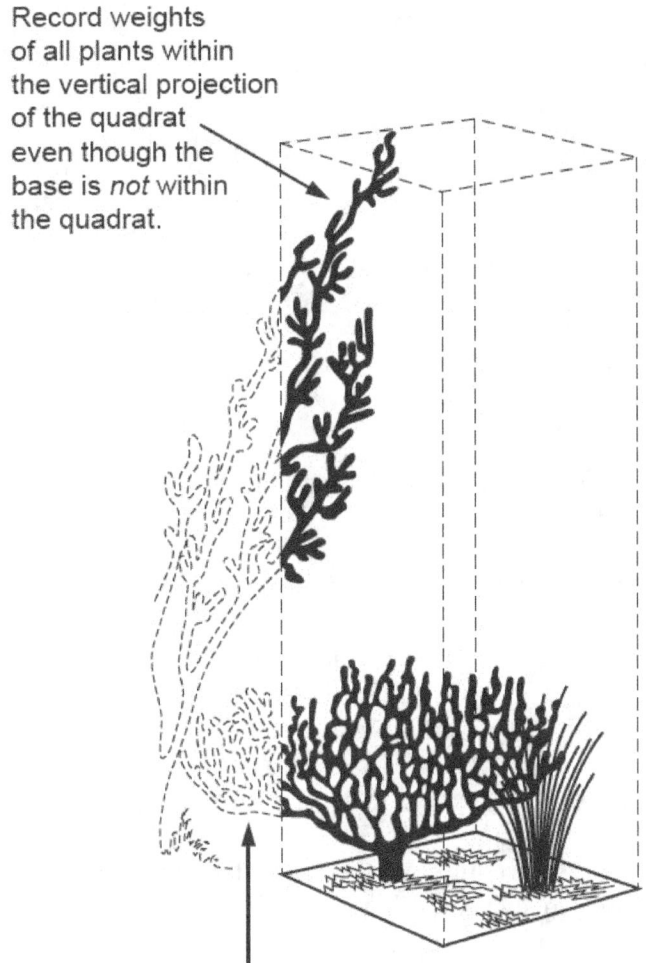

Do not record weights of portions of plants outside the vertical projection of the quadrat even though the base *is* within the quadrat

Illustration 23

111

## K. Harvest Method

1. *General Description* The concept of this method is to determine the amount of current-year above-ground vegetation production on a defined area. The following vegetation attributes are monitored:

   • Peak standing crop, which is the above-ground annual production of each plant species

   • Species composition by weight

   It is important to establish a photo plot (see Section V.A) and take both close-up and general view photographs. This allows the portrayal of resource values and conditions and furnishes visual evidence of vegetation and soil changes over time.

2. *Areas of Use* This method can be used in a wide variety of vegetation types. It is best suited for grasslands and desert shrubs. It is not well suited to large shrub and tree communities.

3. *Advantages and Limitations*

   a  The harvest method measures the attribute historically used to determine the capabilities of an ecosystem.

   b  It provides the basic data currently used for determining ecological status.

   c  Seasonal and annual fluctuations in climate can influence plant biomass.

   d  Measurements can be time-consuming.

   e  Current year's growth can be hard to separate from previous years' growth.

   f  Accurate measurements require collecting production data at peak production periods which, are usually short, or using utilization and phenology adjustment factors.

   g  Green weights require conversion to air-dry weights.

   h  In most areas, the variability in production between quadrats requires the sampling of large numbers of quadrats in order to detect reasonable levels of change.

4. *Equipment* The following equipment is needed (see also the equipment listed in Section V.A, page 31, for the establishment of the photo plot):

   • Study Location and Documentation Data form (see Appendix A)
   • Production form (Illustration 22, page 109)
   • Sampling frames or hoops
   • One stake: 3/4- or 1-inch angle iron not less than 16 inches long
   • Herbage Yield Tables for Trees by Height, DBH, or Canopy

- Clippers
- Paper bags
- Kilogram and gram spring-loaded scales with clip
- Tree diameter measuring tape
- Steel post and driver
- Oven for drying vegetation
- Air-dry weight conversion tables
- Rubber bands
- Compass

5. *Training* The accuracy of the measurement depends on the training and ability of the examiners. Examiners must be able to identify plant species and determine current year's growth.

6. *Establishing Studies* Careful establishment of studies is a critical element in obtaining meaningful data (see Section III).

   a **Site Selection** The most important factor in obtaining usable data is selecting representative areas (critical or key areas) in which to run the study (see Section II.D). Study sites should be located within a single plant community within a single ecological site. Transects and sampling points need to be randomly located within the critical or key areas (see Section III).

      (1) Select transects at random (see Section III.B. 2).

      (2) The number of quadrats selected depends on the purpose for which the estimates are to be used, uniformity of the vegetation, and other factors (see Section III.B for Statistical considerations.)

      (3) Adapt the size and shape of quadrats to the vegetation community to be sampled (see Section III.B.6).

   b **Pilot Studies** Collect data on several pilot studies to determine the number of samples (transects or observation points) and the number and size of quadrats needed to collect a statistically valid sample (see Section III.B.8).

   c **Study Layout** Production data can be collected using either the baseline, macroplot, or linear study designs described in Section III.A.2 beginning on page 8. The linear technique is the one most often used.

   d **Reference Post or Point** Permanently mark the location of each study with a reference post and a study location stake (see beginning of Section III).

   e **Study Identification** Number studies for proper identification to ensure that the data collected can be positively associated with specific sites on the ground (Appendix B).

   f **Study Documentation** Document pertinent information concerning the study on the Study Location and Documentation Data form (see beginning of Section III and Appendix A).

7. *Taking Photographs* The directions for establishing photo plots and for taking close-up and general view photographs are given in Section V.A.

8. *Sampling Process* In addition to collecting the specific studies data, general observations should be made of the study sites (see Section II.F).

   **a** Determine the transect bearing and select a prominent distant landmark such as a peak, rocky point, etc., that can be used as the transect bearing point.

   **b** Randomly select the starting point along the transect bearing. Take the specified number of paces and read the first quadrat.

   **c** Record weights by clipping and weighing all vegetative material for each species occurring in the quadrat. Samples should be bagged and saved for determining air-dry weights. Samples from subsequent quadrats should be kept separate. The following information should be record on each bag: Date, Transect Number, Quadrat Number, and Species.

   When harvesting plants, include all parts of all plants *within* the quadrat. Exclude *all* parts of herbaceous plants and shrubs outside the vertical projection of the quadrat, even though the base is within the quadrat (see Illustration 23).

   **d** Continue the transect by establishing additional quadrats at specified intervals. To change the length of the transect, adjust the number of paces between quadrats.

   **e** Oven-dry samples at 60°C for 24 hours to determine air-dry weight.

9. *Calculations* The weights collected for each species per quadrat placement are recorded on the Production form (see Illustration 22).

   **a** The green weight for each species is totaled for the entire transect and shown in column 5.

   **b** Column 6 is the total dry weight for each species. This column is totaled at the bottom of the form for the composition totals.

   **c** Percent composition (Column 11) is calculated by dividing the total dry weight of each species by the composition totals.

   **d** Columns 4, 7, 8, 9,and 10 are used only for double sampling.

   **e** If plant biomass is collected in grams, it can be easily converted to pounds per acres if the total area sampled is a multiple of 9.6 ft$^2$.

Use the following table to convert grams to pounds per acre:

**Table 5**

(# of plots  x  size  =  total area)

| (10 x 0.96 | = | 9.6 ft² ) | multiply grams times | 10.0 | = | pounds per acre |
|---|---|---|---|---|---|---|
| (10 x 1.92 | = | 19.2 ft² ) | multiply grams times | 5.0 | = | pounds per acre |
| (10 x 2.40 | = | 24.0 ft² ) | multiply grams times | 4.0 | = | pounds per acre |
| (10 x 4.80 | = | 48.0 ft² ) | multiply grams times | 2.0 | = | pounds per acre |
| (10 x 9.60 | = | 96.0 ft² ) | multiply grams times | 1.0 | = | pounds per acre |
| (10 x 96.0 | = | 960.0 ft² ) | multiply grams times | 0.1 | = | pounds per acre |

10. *Data Analysis* This technique involves destructive sampling (clipped plots), so permanent transects or quadrats are not recommended. Since the transects are not permanently marked, use the appropriate nonpaired test. When comparing more than two sampling periods, use ANOVA.

11. *References*

Cook, C. Wayne and James Stubbendieck, 1986. Range Research: Basic Problems and Techniques. Society for Range Management. Denver, CO.

Laycock, W.A. 1987. Setting Objectives and Picking Appropriate Methods for Monitoring Vegetation on Rangelands. Rangeland Monitoring Workshop Proceedings. U.S. Department of Interior. Bureau of Land Management. Golden, CO.

Pechanec, J.F. and G.D. Pickford. 1937. A weight-estimate method for the determination of range or pasture production. J. Amer. Soc. Agron. 29:894-904.

Riser, Paul G. 1984. Methods for Inventory and Monitoring of Vegetation, Litter, and Soil Surface Condition. Developing Strategies for Rangeland Monitoring. National Research Council National Academy of Sciences.

USDA, Soil Conservation Service. 1976. National Range Handbook. 154 p.

USDI, Bureau of Land Management. 1984 (rev. 1990). National Range Handbook 4410-1. Washington D. C.

Van Dyne, George M., W.G. Vogel, and H.G. Fisser. 1963. Influence of small plot size and shape on range herbage production estimates. Ecology 44:746-759.

# L. Comparative Yield Method

1. *General Description* This method is used to estimate total standing crop or production of a site. The total production in a sample quadrat is compared to one of five reference quadrats; relative ranks are recorded rather than estimating the weight directly.

   It is important to establish a photo plot (see Section V.A) and take both close-up and general view photographs. This allows the portrayal of resource values and conditions and furnishes visual evidence of vegetation and soil changes over time.

2. *Areas of Use* This method works best for herbaceous vegetation but can also be used successfully with small shrubs and half-shrubs. As with most production estimates, the comparative yield method can be used to compare relative production between different sites.

3. *Advantages and Limitations* The advantage of the comparative yield method is that a large sample can be obtained quickly. Total production is evaluated, so clipping calibration on a species basis is not needed. The process of developing reference quadrats for ranking purposes reduces both sampling and training time. This technique can be done in conjunction with the frequency, canopy cover, or dry weight rank methods. Identification of individual species is not required.

   Large shrub communities are not well suited for this technique. If used in conjunction with other techniques (frequency and dry weight rank), the quadrat size may need to be different. This technique can detect only large changes in production.

4. *Equipment* The following equipment is needed (see also the equipment listed in Section V.A, page 31, for the establishment of the photo plot):

   - Study Location and Documentation Data form (see Appendix A)
   - Comparative Yield form (Illustration 24)
   - Five sampling quadrat frames
   - Clippers
   - Paper bags
   - Kilogram and gram spring-loaded scale with clip
   - One stake: 3/4- or 1-inch angle iron not less than 16 inches long
   - Tally counter (optional)
   - Hammer
   - Permanent yellow or orange spray paint
   - Compass
   - Steel post and driver

5. *Training* Examiners must calibrate their estimates when sampling situations change (i.e., different sites, time of day, or season).

6. *Establishing Studies* Careful establishment of studies is a critical element in obtaining meaningful data. Depending on the objectives, comparative yield data can be collected on permanent transects or in a random or systematic design.

a **Site Selection** The most important factor in obtaining usable data is selecting representative areas (critical or key areas) in which to run the study (see Section II.D). Study sites should be located within a single plant community within a single ecological site. Transects and sampling points need to be randomly located within the critical or key areas (see Section III).

b **Pilot Studies** Collect data on several pilot studies to determine the number of samples (transects or observation points) and the number and size of quadrats needed to collect a statistically valid sample (see Section III.B.8).

c **Selecting Quadrat Size** The criteria for selecting the proper size quadrat is the same as any weight estimate procedure (see Section III.B.6.d).

   (1) Determine the proper size quadrat(s) to use by doing preliminary sampling with different size frames.

   (2) Use the same size quadrat throughout a study and for rereading the study.

d **Number of Transects** Establish one transect on each study site; establish more if needed.

e **Study Layout** Production data can be collected using the baseline, macroplot, or linear study designs described in Section III.A.2 beginning on page 8. The linear technique is the one most often used.

f **Reference Post or Point** Permanently mark the location of each study with a reference post and a study location stake (see beginning of Section III).

g **Study Identification** Number studies for proper identification to ensure that the data collected can be positively associated with specific sites on the ground (see Appendix B).

h **Study Documentation** Document pertinent information concerning the study on the Study Location and Documentation Data form (see beginning of Section III and Appendix A).

7. *Taking Photographs* The directions for establishing photo plots and for taking close-up and general view photographs are given in Section V.A.

8. *Sampling Process* In addition to collecting the specific study data, general observations should be made of the study sites (see Section II.F).

   a A set of reference quadrats must be established. The sample quadrats will be compared and rated back to these reference quadrats. The reference quadrats represent the range in dry weight of standing crop that will be commonly found during sampling.

(1) Five reference quadrats are subjectively located. References 1 and 5 are located first. The first quadrat (reference 1) is placed in a low-yielding area which represents the low-yielding situations commonly encountered on the site (avoid bare or nearly bare quadrats). Reference 5 is determined by placing a quadrat on a high-yielding area, excluding unusually dense patches of vegetation which would have a rare chance of being sampled. The examiner should make a mental note of the amount of production in each of the reference quadrats. These references are then clipped and weighed. If the clipped weight in reference 5 is more than five times the weight found in reference 1, then two new sites should be selected as references 1 and 5. In establishing the initial reference quadrats, the weight in reference 5 is usually too high and the weight in reference 1 is too low. Make sure reference 5 does not represent a rare situation. When references 1 and 5 have been selected, reference 3 is located by placing a frame in an area considered to have a yield halfway between references 1 and 5. References 2 and 4 are located the same way by selecting the mid-point yield between references 1 and 3 and references 3 and 5, respectively.

(2) All five reference quadrats are clipped and weighed to compare the reference quadrats to a linear distribution of quadrat weights. This process is repeated by clipping additional quadrats until the weights of the five reference quadrats are approximately linear and observers are confident in their ability to rank quadrats relative to one of the five references. If the rankings are not linear, the precision of the method will be reduced. If more than five percent of the quadrats have no production, then a larger quadrat frame should be used.

(3) In areas with less than 500 lb/ac, small quadrats are difficult to evaluate. In these situations, larger quadrats should be used or three reference quadrats should be established instead of five.

## b  Collecting the Data

(1) Start a transect by randomly locating the first quadrat along the transect bearing.

(2) Read additional quadrats at specified intervals. To change the length of the transect, increase the number of paces between quadrats.

(3) For each quadrat, compare the total yield in the quadrat to the references and record the appropriate rank by dot count tally. It is appropriate to assign intermediate ranks if the yield is at the midpoint between two references. For example, if a quadrat has a yield between references 1 and 2, assign a rank of 1.5. If a quadrat yield greatly exceeds the yield of reference 5, then a higher rank may be estimated. For example, if a quadrat is 50% greater than reference 5, a rank of 7 could be recorded. If more than five percent of the quadrats are ranked above 5, the references were not properly selected.

(4) To calibrate the ranks, several quadrats representing each reference should be clipped and weighed independently of the transect. The total yield in

each quadrat is determined without regard to species. Be sure to save all clipped material. The reference quadrats can be used as part of these clipped quadrats. The more quadrats clipped, the better the calibration. Each distinct sampling period should have a separate calibration. Bags can be weighed in the field to determine green weight and then saved and dried to determine dry weight (see Section V.J.9.b.(6)). These weights are then used to determine average weight per reference.

9. *Calculations* The number of quadrats tallied for each ranking is totaled (Illustration 7, column 2) and multiplied by the ranking (column 1).

$$\text{Rank x Tally} = \text{Weighted ranking}$$

These weighted rankings (column 3) are summed and divided by the number of total quadrats. This indicates the average ranking for the site.

$$\frac{\text{Total rank}}{\text{Total number of quadrats sampled}} = \text{Average ranking for the site}$$

The average yield may be estimated with a ratio estimate (described below) or a least-squares regression technique. The ratio estimate is good for quick field calculations, but the least-squares regression should be used for final data analysis.

To use the ratio estimate technique, calculate the average rank and average clipped weight of the harvested quadrats by dividing the total of the clipped rankings and the total clipped weight by the number of harvested (clipped) quadrats (column 4 and 5).

$$\frac{\text{Total of clipped rankings}}{\text{Total number of clipped quadrats}} = \text{Average rank of clipped quadrats}$$

$$\frac{\text{Total clipped weight}}{\text{Total number of clipped quadrats}} = \text{Average weight of clipped quadrats}$$

The average clipped weight is then divided by the average rank to determine the average rank interval.

$$\frac{\text{Average weight of clipped quadrats}}{\text{Average rank of clipped quadrats}} = \text{Average rank interval (ARI)}$$

The average ranking for the site—which is based on the *estimated*, not clipped, quadrats—is then multiplied by the average rank interval to estimate the average yield per quadrat for the site.

$$\text{Average ranking for the site } \mathbf{x} \text{ Average rank interval} = \text{Average yield/Quadrat.}$$

The average yield in grams per quadrat obtained above can be converted to either pounds/acre or kilograms/hectare.

Use the following table to convert grams to pounds per acre if the total area sampled is a multiple of 9.6 ft$^2$.

**Table 6**

(# of plots  x  size  =  total area)

| | | | | | | | | |
|---|---|---|---|---|---|---|---|---|
| (10 x 0.96 | = | 9.6 ft²) | multiply grams times | 10.0 | = | pounds per acre |
| (10 x 1.92 | = | 19.2 ft²) | multiply grams times | 5.0 | = | pounds per acre |
| (10 x 2.40 | = | 24.0 ft²) | multiply grams times | 4.0 | = | pounds per acre |
| (10 x 4.80 | = | 48.0 ft²) | multiply grams times | 2.0 | = | pounds per acre |
| (10 x 9.60 | = | 96.0 ft²) | multiply grams times | 1.0 | = | pounds per acre |
| (10 x 96.0 | = | 960.0 ft²) | multiply grams times | 0.1 | = | pounds per acre |

To convert to kilograms per hectare, first determine the number of quadrats in a hectare by dividing the number of square meters in a hectare ($10,000m^2$) by the total area (in square meters) of the quadrat. Then divide the number of quadrats in a hectare by 1,000 to arrive at the conversion factor used to convert grams per quadrat into kilograms per hectare.

For example, if the quadrat size is 40 X 40 centimeters (0.4 X 0.4 meters), then the quadrat area would be 0.4 multiplied by 0.4, or $.16m^2$. The number of quadrats in a hectare is calculated by dividing 10,000 by .16, which works out to 62,500 quadrats per acre. Dividing this number by 1,000 results in the conversion factor, which is 62.5. The final step is to multiply the average yield per quadrat obtained from the final equation above by 62.5 to arrive at kilograms per hectare.

10. *Data Analysis*  For trend analysis, permanent sampling units are suggested. If permanent transects are monitored, use the appropriate paired analysis technique. If the transects are not permanently marked, use the appropriate nonpaired test. When comparing more than two sampling periods, use repeated measures ANOVA.

11. *References*

Despain, D.W., P.R. Ogden, and E.L. Smith. 1991. Plant frequency sampling for monitoring rangelands. In: G.B. Ruyle, ed. Some Methods for Monitoring Rangelands and other Natural Area Vegetation. Extension Report 9043, University of Arizona, College of Agriculture, Tucson, AZ.

## Comparative Yield

| Study Number | | Date | Examiner | | Pasture |
|---|---|---|---|---|---|
| Allotment Name & Number | | | Number of Quadrats | | Quadrat Size |
| Study Location | | | | | |

| Sampled Quadrats | | | Harvested Quadrat | |
|---|---|---|---|---|
| Rank (1) | Tally (2) | Rank x Tally (3) | Clip Rank (4) | Clip Weight (5) |
| 0 | | | | |
| .5 | | | | |
| 1 | | | | |
| 1.5 | | | | |
| 2 | | | | |
| 2.5 | | | | |
| 3 | | | | |
| 3.5 | | | | |
| 4 | | | | |
| 4.5 | | | | |
| 5 | | | | |
| | | | | |
| | | | | |
| | | | | |
| | | | | |
| | | | | |
| | | | | |
| | | | | |
| | | | | |
| | | | | |
| | | | | |
| | | | | |
| Total | | | | |
| Average | | | | |

Notes

Illustration 24    121

## Comparative Yield

| Study Number | Date | Examiner | Pasture |
|---|---|---|---|
| Silver Creek #4 | 8/9/95 | Wally Pip | 3 |

| Allotment Name & Number | Number of Quadrats | Quadrat Size |
|---|---|---|
| Silver Creek 21703 | 25 | 40 × 40 |

Study Location  2 miles EAST of Red Well on NORTH side of road.

| Sampled Quadrats | | | Harvested Quadrat | |
|---|---|---|---|---|
| Rank (1) | Tally (2) | Rank x Tally (3) | Clip Rank (4) | Clip Weight (5) |
| 0 | 0 | 0 | 1 | 10 |
| .5 | 0 | 0 | 2 | 27 |
| 1 | 3 | 3 | 3 | 46 |
| 1.5 | 4 | 6 | 4 | 62 |
| 2 | 5 | 10 | 5 | 83 |
| 2.5 | 4 | 10 | | |
| 3 | 2 | 6 | | |
| 3.5 | 3 | 10.5 | | |
| 4 | 2 | 8 | | |
| 4.5 | 1 | 4.5 | | |
| 5 | 1 | 5 | | |
| | | | | |
| | | | | |
| | | | | |
| | | | | |
| | | | | |
| | | | | |
| | | | | |
| | | | | |
| | | | | |
| | | | | |
| | | | | |
| | | | | |
| Total | 25 | 63 | 15 | 228 |
| Average | | 2.52 | 3 | 45.6 |

Notes

Illustration 24

# M. Visual Obstruction Method - Robel Pole

1. *General Description* This method is used for determining standing plant biomass on an area. It has primarily been used to determine the quality of nesting cover for birds on the Great Plains and is commonly referred to as the Robel Pole Method. This method is applicable to other ecosystems throughout the western U.S. where height and vertical obstruction of cover are important. The following vegetation attributes are monitored using this method:

   - Vertical cover
   - Production
   - Structure

   It is important to establish a photo plot (see Section V.A) and take both close-up and general view photographs. This allows the portrayal of resource values and conditions and furnishes visual evidence of vegetation and soil changes over time.

2. *Areas of Use* The Robel Pole Method is most effective in upland and riparian areas where perennial grasses, forbs, and shrubs less than 4 feet tall are the predominant species.

3. *Advantages and Disadvantages* Robel Pole measurements are simple, quick, and accurate. This method can be used to monitor height and density of standing vegetation over large areas quickly. Statistical reliability improves because numerous measurements can be taken in a relatively short time. Limitations of the method may stem from infrequent application in a variety of rangeland ecosystems. While the Robel Pole Method has been used with great success on the Great Plains, there needs to be more research in a variety of plant communities.

4. *Equipment* The following equipment is needed (see also the equipment listed in Section V.A, page 31, for the establishment of the photo plot):

   - Study Location and Documentation Data form (see Appendix A)
   - Robel Pole form (Illustration 25)
   - Cover classes for the area or plant community
   - Robel pole (Illustration 26)
   - One stake: 3/4- or 1-inch angle iron not less than 16 inches long
   - Hammer
   - Permanent yellow or orange spray paint
   - Compass
   - Steel post and driver

5. *Training* The accuracy of the data depends on the training and ability of the examiners. They must receive adequate and consistent training in laying out transects, determining cover classes, and reading the Robel pole.

6. *Establishing Studies* Careful establishment of studies is a critical element in obtaining meaningful data. Select study sites that are representative of much larger areas in terms of similar cover levels.

a **Site Selection** The most important factor in obtaining usable data is selecting representative areas (critical or key areas) in which to run the study (see Section II.D). Study sites should be located within a single plant community within a single ecological site. Transects and sampling points need to be randomly located within the critical or key areas (see Section III).

b **Pilot Studies** Collect data on several pilot studies to determine the number of samples (transects or observation points) and the number and size of quadrats needed to collect a statistically valid sample (see Section III.B.8).

c **Vertical Cover Classes** Establish the number of vertical cover classes and height limits for each class based on objectives. These cover classes must be developed locally for each ecological site or plant community. The following is an example of cover classes established for upland bird nesting cover on the Fort Pierre National Grasslands:

| Cover Classes | Visual Obstruction Height |
|:---:|:---:|
| 1 | 0.0 - 1.9 |
| 2 | 2.0 - 2.9 |
| 3 | 3.0 - 3.9 |
| 4 | 4.0 + |

d **Number of Transects** Establish the minimum number of transects to achieve the desired level of precision for the key species in each study site (see Section III.B).

e **Number of Observation Points** The number of observation points will depend on the objectives, level of precision required, etc.; however, it is recommended that a *minimum* of 50 be read per transect. Additional observation points should be read, depending on the pilot study.

f **Study Layout** Data can be collected using the baseline, macroplot, or linear study designs described in Section III.A.2 beginning on page 8. The linear technique is the one most often used.

g **Reference Post or Point** Permanently mark the location of each study with a reference post and a study location stake (see beginning of Section III).

h **Study Identification** Number studies for proper identification to ensure that the data collected can be positively associated with specific sites on the ground (see Appendix B).

i **Study Documentation** Document pertinent information concerning the study on the Study Location and Documentation Data form (see beginning of Section III and Appendix A).

7. *Taking Photographs* The directions for establishing photo plots and for taking close-up and general view photographs are given in Section V.A.

8. *Sampling Process* In addition to collecting the specific studies data, general observations should be made of the study sites (see Section II.F).

This technique is most effectively accomplished with two individuals.

   a Determine the transect bearing and select a prominent distant landmark such as a peak, rocky point, etc., that can be used as the transect bearing point.

   b Start a transect by randomly selecting a point along the transect. Two Visual Obstruction (VO) measurements are taken at each observation point from opposite directions along the contour. One examiner holds the Robel pole at the observation point, while the second examiner holds the end of the cord perpendicular to the transect. The Visual Observation (VO) measurement is made by determining the highest 1-inch band totally or partially visible and recording the height on the Robel Pole form (Illustration 25).

   c Continue the transect by taking readings at specified intervals along the transect bearing until the transect is complete. The distance between observation points can be increased to expand the area sampled.

9. *Calculations*

   a Total the visual obstruction measurements on the Robel Pole form (Illustration 25) for both readings at each observation point and record at the bottom of the form. Add these two totals and divide by the total number of readings. This will yield the average visual obstruction.

   b The average height or visual obstruction value can be used to determine the cover class.

10. *Production* Data from the Robel pole method can be correlated to forage production or standing crop. This correlation can be established by clipping and weighing the standing crop within a specified quadrat frame directly in front of the Robel pole after the readings are made. Depending on the vegetation community approximately 25 quadrat frames need to be clipped to get a good correlation between visual obstruction readings and standing crop. Note that this will be an estimate of standing plant biomass. It will include not only this year's production, but also herbage remaining from prior years. After the correlation is made between the pole readings and production, the pole can then be used to quickly estimate production across the entire plant community.

11. *Data Interpretation* The average Visual Obstruction value can be used to determine success at meeting objectives. The average Visual Obstruction value determined from the Robel Method form is compared with the cover classes and the residue levels to determine if overall objectives have been meet.

12. *Data Analysis* This technique involves destructive sampling (clipped plots), so permanent transects or quadrats are not recommended. Since the transects are not permanently marked, use the appropriate nonpaired test. When comparing more than two sampling periods, use ANOVA.

## 13. References

Robel, R.J., J.N. Briggs, A.D. Dayton, and L.C. Hulbert. 1970. Relationships Between Visual Obstruction Measurements and Weight of Grassland Vegetation, J. Range Manage. 23:295.

Robel, R.J. 1970. Possible Role of Behavior in Regulating Greater Prairie Chicken's Populations, J. Wildlife Manage. Vol 34:306-312.

Snyder, W.D. 1991. Wheat stubble as nesting cover for ring necked pheasants in northern Colorado. Wildlife Soc. bulletin vol 19(4).

USDA, Forest Service. 1994. Rangeland Analysis and Management Training Guide, Rocky Mountain Region USDA Forest Service Denver, Colorado.

# Robel Pole

| Study Number | | | Date | | Examiner | | |
|---|---|---|---|---|---|---|---|

| Allotment Name & Number | | | | Pasture | | | |
|---|---|---|---|---|---|---|---|

| Sampling Interval | | Study Location | | | | | |
|---|---|---|---|---|---|---|---|

| Transect | #- 1 | | #- | | #- | | #- | |
|---|---|---|---|---|---|---|---|---|
| Station | VO | VO | VO | VO | VO | VO | VO | VO |
| 1 | | | | | | | | |
| 2 | | | | | | | | |
| 3 | | | | | | | | |
| 4 | | | | | | | | |
| 5 | | | | | | | | |
| 6 | | | | | | | | |
| 7 | | | | | | | | |
| 8 | | | | | | | | |
| 9 | | | | | | | | |
| 10 | | | | | | | | |
| 11 | | | | | | | | |
| 12 | | | | | | | | |
| 13 | | | | | | | | |
| 14 | | | | | | | | |
| 15 | | | | | | | | |
| 16 | | | | | | | | |
| 17 | | | | | | | | |
| 18 | | | | | | | | |
| 19 | | | | | | | | |
| 20 | | | | | | | | |
| 21 | | | | | | | | |
| 22 | | | | | | | | |
| 23 | | | | | | | | |
| 24 | | | | | | | | |
| 25 | | | | | | | | |
| Total | | | | | | | | |
| Grand Total | | | | | | | | |
| Average | | | | | | | | |

**Illustration 25**     127

## Robel Pole

| Study Number | Sand Hill #1 | | | Date | 6/18/94 | | Examiner | Scott Taylor | |
|---|---|---|---|---|---|---|---|---|---|

| Allotment Name & Number | Sand Hill 20216 | | | Pasture | 2 | | | | |
|---|---|---|---|---|---|---|---|---|---|

| Sampling Interval | 10 paces | | Study Location | 2 mi. west of Walker Well on south side of the road. | | | | | |
|---|---|---|---|---|---|---|---|---|---|

| Transect | #- 1 | | #- | | #- | | #- | | |
|---|---|---|---|---|---|---|---|---|
| Station | VO | VO | VO | VO | VO | VO | VO | VO |
| 1 | 1 | 3 | | | | | | |
| 2 | 2 | 4 | | | | | | |
| 3 | 1 | 1 | | | | | | |
| 4 | 2 | 1 | | | | | | |
| 5 | 3 | 1 | | | | | | |
| 6 | 1 | 2 | | | | | | |
| 7 | 3 | 4 | | | | | | |
| 8 | 3 | 3 | | | | | | |
| 9 | 4 | 4 | | | | | | |
| 10 | 1 | 2 | | | | | | |
| 11 | 2 | 3 | | | | | | |
| 12 | 1 | 1 | | | | | | |
| 13 | 2 | 1 | | | | | | |
| 14 | 3 | 2 | | | | | | |
| 15 | 2 | 3 | | | | | | |
| 16 | 1 | 2 | | | | | | |
| 17 | 2 | 2 | | | | | | |
| 18 | 3 | 3 | | | | | | |
| 19 | 2 | 4 | | | | | | |
| 20 | 3 | 3 | | | | | | |
| 21 | 3 | 2 | | | | | | |
| 22 | 1 | 3 | | | | | | |
| 23 | 2 | 2 | | | | | | |
| 24 | 3 | 1 | | | | | | |
| 25 | 2 | 2 | | | | | | |
| Total | 53 | 59 | | | | | | |
| Grand Total | 112 | | | | | | | |
| Average | 2.24 | | | | | | | |

Illustration 25

# Robel Pole

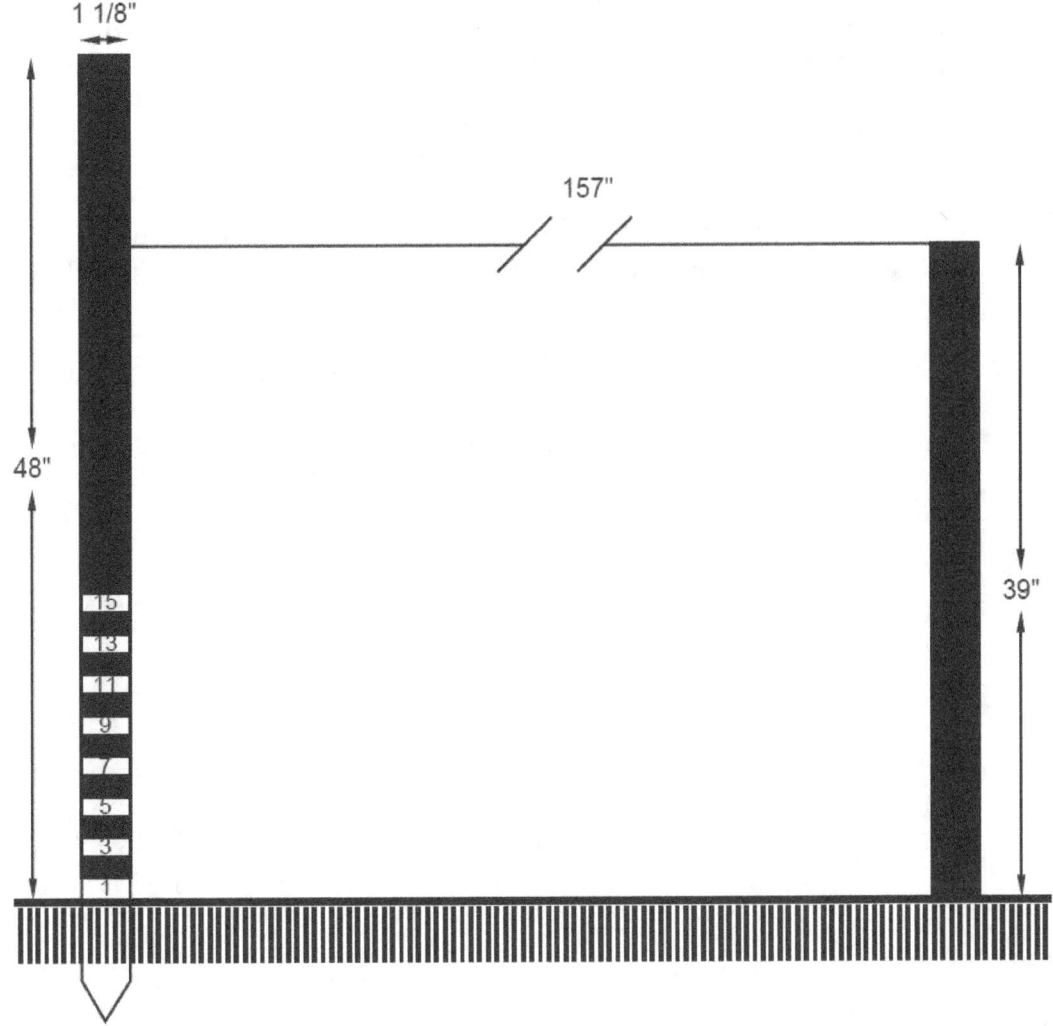

1. Pole is 1.125 inches in diameter and 48 inches long.

2. Pole is painted with alternating 1-inch bands of flat white and gray colors, starting with white on the bottom. Alternating 1-inch bands can be extended to the top of the pole if needed.

3. A single 157-inch (4m) cord is attached to the pole at a height of 39 inches (1m) to standardize the distance and height at which readings are taken.

4. Narrow black numbers corresponding to the number of bands are painted on the white bands. For example, the bottom white band is "1," the next white band is "3," and so on.

5. A spike is attached to the bottom of the pole so that it can be pushed into the ground, allowing one examiner to make the readings. The spike can be removed if not needed.

Illustration 26

129

# N. Other Methods

1. *Weight Estimate and Ocular Reconnaissance Methods* Both of these methods were commonly used to determine forage production prior to the implementation of the Ecological Site Inventory Method. They both involved determining the production on all species, which could then be used to calculate species composition and total production. Although they are no longer widely used techniques, written description for completing each can be found in BLM's *Rangeland Inventory and Monitoring Supplemental Studies,* Technical Reference 4400-5.

2. *Community Structure Analysis Method* This technique is used by very few field offices. It will be moved to BLM's Technical Reference 4400-5 in a future revision.

3. *Photo Plot Method* This technique requires many quadrats for each study site in order to provide statistically reliable data. Since this technique is very time consuming, it is no longer used in most field offices. It will be moved to BLM's Technical Reference 4400-5 in a future revision.

# VI. GLOSSARY OF TERMS

## A

**actual use:** a report of the actual livestock grazing use certified to be accurate by the permittee or lessee. Actual use may be expressed in terms of animal unit months or animal months.

**allotment:** an area of land designated and managed for grazing by livestock. Such an area may include intermingled private, state, or federal lands used for grazing in conjunction with the public lands.

**allotment management plan (AMP):** a documented program which applies to livestock grazing on the public lands, prepared by consulting, cooperating, and coordinating with the permittee(s), lessee(s), or other interested publics.

**analysis:** (1) a detailed examination of anything complex in order to understand its nature or determine its essential features; or (2) a separating or breaking up of any whole into its component parts for the purpose of examining their nature, function, relationship, etc. A rangeland analysis includes an examination of both biotic (plants, animals, etc.) and abiotic (soils, topography, etc.) attributes of the rangeland.

**annual plant:** a plant that completes its life cycle and dies in 1 year or less.

**animal month:** a month's tenure upon the rangeland by one animal. Animal month is not synonymous with animal unit month.

**animal unit:** considered to be one mature cow of approximately 1,000 pounds, either dry or with calf up to six months of age, or their equivalent, based on a standardized amount of forage consumed.

**animal unit month (AUM):** the amount of dry forage required by one animal unit for one month, based on a forage allowance of 26 pounds per day.

**apparent trend:** an assessment, using professional judgement, based on a one-time observation. It includes consideration of such factors as plant vigor, abundance of seedlings and young plants, accumulation or lack of plant residues on the soil surface, and soil surface characteristics (i.e., crusting, gravel pavement, pedicled plants, and sheet or rill erosion.

**available forage:** that portion of the forage production that is accessible for use by a specified kind or class of grazing animal.

## B

**basal cover (area):** the cross-sectional area of the stem or stems of a plant, or all plants in a stand. Herbaceous and small woody plants are measured at or near the ground level; larger woody plants are measured at breast or other designated height.

**biomass:** the total amount of living plants and animals above and below ground in an area at a given time.

**browse:** (1) the part of shrubs, half shrubs, woody vines, and trees available for animal consumption; or (2) to search for or consume browse.

**browse plant or browse species:** a shrub, half shrub, woody vine, or tree capable of producing shoot, twig, and leaf growth suitable for animal consumption.

# C

**canopy cover:** the percentage of ground covered by a vertical projection of the outermost perimeter of the natural spread of foliage of plants. Small openings within the canopy are included. Canopy cover is synonymous with crown cover.

**class of livestock:** the age and/or sex groups of a kind of livestock.

**community:** an assemblage of populations of plants and/or animals in a common spatial arrangement.

**composition:** the proportions of various plant species in relation to the total on a given area. It may be expressed in terms of relative cover, relative density, relative weight, etc.

**cool season species:** plants whose major growth occurs during the late fall, winter and early spring.

**crown cover:** (See canopy cover.)

**critical area:** an area which should be treated with special consideration because of inherent site factors, size, location, condition, values, or significant potential conflicts among uses.

# D

**density:** numbers of individuals or stems per unit area (does not equate to any kind of cover measurement).

# E

**ecological site:** a kind of rangeland with a specific potential natural community and specific physical site characteristics, differing from other kinds of rangeland in its ability to produce vegetation and to respond to management. Ecological sites are defined and described with soil, species composition, and production emphasis. Ecological site is synonymous with range site and ecological type (FS).

**ecological status:** the present state of vegetation of an ecological site in relation to the potential natural community for the site. Ecological status is independent of use. It is an expression of the relative degree to which the kinds, proportions, and amounts of plants in a community resemble that of the potential natural community. The four ecological status classes correspond to 0-25, 26-50, 51-75, or 76-100 percent similarity to the potential natural community and are called *early-seral, mid-seral, late-seral,* and *potential natural community,* respectively.

**estimated use:** the use made of forage on an area by wildlife, wild horses, wild burros, and/ or livestock where actual use data are not available. Estimated use may be expressed in terms of animal unit months or animal months.

**evaluation:** (1) an examination and judgment concerning the worth, quality, significance, amount, degree, or condition of something; or (2) the systematic process for determining the effectiveness of on-the-ground management actions and assessing progress toward meeting objectives.

# F

**foliar cover:** the percentage of ground covered by a downward vertical projection of the aerial portion of plant foliage, excluding small openings in the canopy,  Foliar cover is always less than canopy cover.  Total  foliar cover of all species may exceed 100 percent.

**forage:** (1) browse and herbage which is available and can provide food for animals or be harvested for feeding; or (2) to search for or consume forage.

**forage production:** the weight of forage that is produced within a designated period of time or a given area.  Production may be expressed as green, air dry, or oven dry weight.  The term may also be modified as to time of production such as annual, current year, or seasonal forage production.

**forb:** (1) any herbaceous plant other than those in the Gramineae (true grasses), Cyperaceae (sedges), and Juncaceae (rushes) families—i.e., any nongrass-like plant having little or no woody material on it; or (2) a broadleaved flowering plant whose above-ground stem does not become woody and persistent.

**forestland:** land on which the vegetation is dominated by trees.  Lands are classified forest-land if the trees now present will provide 25 percent or greater canopy cover at maturity. Lands not presently forestland that were originally or could become forested through natural succession may be classified as potential natural forestland.

**frequency:** a quantitative expression of the presence or absence of individuals of a species in a population.  It is defined as the percentage of occurrence of a species in a series of samples of uniform size.

# G

**goal:** the desired state or condition that a resource management policy or program is de-signed to achieve.  A goal is usually not quantifiable and may not have a specific date by which it is to be completed.  Goals are the base from which objectives are developed. (See objective.)

**grass:** any plant of the family Gramineae.

**grassland:** land on which the vegetation is dominated by grasses, grasslike plants, and/or forbs.  Non-forested lands are classified as grassland if herbaceous vegetation provides at least 80 percent of the canopy cover excluding trees.  Lands not presently grassland that were originally or could become grassland through natural succession may be classified as potential natural grassland.

**grasslike plant:** a plant of the Cyperaceae or Juncaceae families which vegetatively re-sembles a true grass of the Gramineae family.

**grazable woodland:** forestland on which the understory includes, as an integral part of the forest plant community, plants that can be grazed without detrimental impact to other forest values.

**ground cover:** The percentage of material, other than bare ground covering the land surface. It may include live and standing dead vegetation, litter cobble, gravel, stones, and bedrock. Ground cover plus bare ground would total 100 percent.

# H

**half shrub:** a plant with a woody base whose annually produced stems die each year.

**herbaceous:** vegetation growth with little or no woody component; nonwoody vegetation such as graminoids and forbs.

**hedging:** (1) the appearance of browse plants that have been browsed so as to appear artificially clipped; or (2) consistent browsing of terminal buds of browse species that results in excessive lateral branching and a reduction in upward and outward growth.

**herbage:** the above-ground material of any herbaceous plant (grasses and forbs).

# I

**interpretation:** explaining or telling the meaning of something and presenting it in understandable terms.

**inventory:** the systematic acquisition and analysis of information needed to describe, characterize, or quantify resources for land-use planning and management of the public lands.

# K

**key area:** a relatively small portion of a range selected because of its location, use or grazing value as a monitoring point for grazing use. It is assumed that key areas, if properly selected, will reflect the overall acceptability of current grazing management over the range.

**key species:** (1) forage species whose use serves as an indicator to the degree of use of associated species. (2) those species which must, because of their importance, be considered in the management program.

**kind of livestock:** species of domestic livestock—cattle, sheep, horses, burros, and goats.

# L

**life-form:** characteristic form or appearance of a species at maturity, e.g., tree, shrub, herb, etc.

# M

**monitoring:** the orderly collection, analysis, and interpretation of resource data to evaluate progress toward meeting objectives.

# N

**native pasture:** land on which native vegetation (climax or natural potential plant community) is forest but which is used and managed primarily for production of native plants for forage. Native pasture includes cutover forest land and forested areas that were cleared and used as cropland.

# O

**objective:** planned results to be achieved within a stated time period. Objectives are subordinate to goals, are narrower in scope and shorter in range, and have increased possibility of attainment. The time periods for completion, and the outputs or achievements that are measurable and quantifiable, are specified. (See goal.)

**overstory:** the upper canopy or canopies of plant, usually referring to trees, shrubs, and vines.

# P

**pasture:** a grazing area enclosed and separated from other areas by a fence or natural barrier.

**potential natural community (PNC):** the biotic community that would become established if all successional sequences were completed without interference by human beings under the present environmental conditions. Natural disturbances are inherent in development. PNCs can include naturalized non-native species.

**proper use:** (1) a degree of utilization of current year's growth which, if continued, will achieve objectives and maintain or improve the long-term productivity of the site; or (2) the percentage of a plant that is utilized when the rangeland as a whole is properly utilized. Proper use varies with time and systems of grazing. Proper use is synonymous with proper utilization.

**public lands:** any land and interest in land outside of Alaska owned by the United States and administered by the Secretary of the Interior through the Bureau of Land Management (see 43 CFR 4100.0-5).

# R

**rangeland:** a kind of land on which the native vegetation is predominantly grasses, grass-like plants, forbs, or shrubs. Includes lands revegetated naturally or artificially when routine management of that vegetation is through manipulation of grazing. Rangelands include natural grasslands, savannas, shrublands, most deserts, tundra, alpine communities, coastal marshes, and wet meadows.

**range site:** (See ecological site.)

**riparian zone:** the banks and adjacent areas of water bodies, water courses, seeps, and springs whose waters provide soil moisture sufficiently in excess of that otherwise available locally so as to provide a more moist habitat than that of contiguous flood plains and uplands.

**rock fragment:** an individual fragment of solid mineral material which occurs naturally on the earth's crust and ranges in size from gravel to boulder.

# S

**sample:** a set of sampling units, as opposed to a single measurement.

**sampling unit:** units on which observations are made. They could be a finite point, plots or quadrats, distance measures, a weight unit, or a transect.

**savanna:** a grassland with scattered trees, whether as individuals or clumps; often a transitional type between true grassland and forest.

**seral community:** one of a series of biotic communities that follow one another in time on any given area. Seral community is synonymous with successional community.

**seral stage:** the developmental stages of an ecological succession; synonymous with successional stage.

**shrub:** a plant that has persistent woody stems and a relatively low growth habit, and that generally produces several basal shoots instead of a single bole. It differs from a tree by its low stature—less than 5 meters (16 feet)—and nonarborescent form.

**shrubland:** land on which the vegetation is dominated by shrubs. Nonforested lands are classified as shrubland if shrubs provide more than 20 percent of the canopy cover, excluding trees. Lands not presently shrubland that were originally or could become shrubland through natural succession may be classified as potential natural shrubland.

**special status plant:** a species that is either Federally listed as threatened or endangered, officially proposed (or a candidate) for Federal listing as threatened or endangered, State listed as threatened or endangered, or listed by a BLM State Director as sensitive.

**stone:** descriptive term applied to rock fragment ground cover where the longest dimension is greater than 10 inches.

**stratification:** subdividing an area into units which are, more or less, internally homogeneous with respect to the (those) characteristic(s) of interest.

**succession:** the orderly process of community change; it is the sequence of communities that replace one another in a given area.

**successional community:** (See seral community.)

**successional stage:** (See seral stage.)

# T

**tree:** a woody perennial, usually single-stemmed plant that has a definite crown shape and characteristically reaches a mature height of at least 5 meters (16 feet). Some plants, such as oaks (Quercus spp.), may grow as either trees or shrubs.

**trend:** the direction of change in ecological status or in resource value ratings observed over time. Trend in ecological status is described as "toward" or "away from" the potential natural community or as "not apparent." Appropriate terms are used to describe trends in resource value ratings. Trends in resource value ratings for several uses on the same site at a given time may be in different directions, and there is no necessary correlation between trends in resource value ratings and the trend in ecological status.

# U

**understory:** plants growing beneath the canopy of other plants; usually refers to grasses, forbs, and low shrubs under a tree or shrub canopy.

**unsuitable rangeland:** rangeland which has no potential value for, or which should not be used for, a specific use because of permanent physical or biological restrictions. When unsuitable rangeland is identified, the identification must specify what use or uses are unsuitable (e.g., "unsuitable for cattle grazing").

**useable forage:** that portion of forage that can be grazed without damage to the basic resources; may vary with season of use, species, and associated species.

**utilization:** the proportion or degree of the current year's forage production by weight that is consumed or destroyed by animals (including insects). The term may refer either to a single plant species, a group of species, or the vegetation community as a whole. Utilization is synonymous with use.

# V

**vegetation:** plants in general, or the sum total of the plant life above and below ground in an area.

**vegetation hit:** a point on vegetation, either basal or canopy, where the tip of the pin or the crosshairs in a sighting device intersect a leaf, stem, or other portion of the plant. Lichens and mosses must exceed 1/16 of an inch in thickness to qualify as a vegetation hit. Lichens and mosses less than 1/16-inch in thickness growing on rock are considered as rock; if they are growing on bare ground, they are considered as persistent litter.

**vegetation type:** a kind of existing plant community with distinguishable characteristics described in terms of the present vegetation that dominates the aspect or physiognomy of the area.

**vigor:** relates to the relative robustness of a plant in comparison to other individuals of the same species. It is reflected primarily by the size of a plant and its parts in relation to its age and the environment in which it is growing.

# W

**warm season species:** plants whose major growth occurs during the spring, summer, or fall and that are usually dormant in winter.

**wet meadow:** a meadow where the surface remains wet or moist throughout the summer, usually characterized by sedges and rushes.

# VII. REFERENCES

Barrett, James P. and Mary E. Nutt. 1979. Survey sampling in the environmental sciences: a computer approach. COMPress, Inc., Wentworth, NH. 319 p.

Biswell, H.H. 1956. Ecology of California grasslands. J. Range Manage. 9:19-24.

Blaisdell, James P. 1958. Seasonal development and yield of native plants on the upper Snake River plains and their relation to certain climatic factors. U.S. Dept. of Agr., For. Ser., Tech. Bul. No. 1190. 68 p.

Bonham, C.D. 1989. Measurements for Terrestrial Vegetation, John Wiley and Sons, 338 p.

Brown, Dorothy. 1954. Methods of surveying and measuring vegetation. Commonwealth Bureau of Pastures and Field Crops. Bulletin No. 42. Commonw. Agr. Bur., Farmham Royal, Bucks, England. 223 p.

Brown, B.W., C. Brauner, A. Chan, D. Gutierrez, J. Herson, J. Lovato, and J. Polsley. 1993. STPLAN, Version 4.0. University of Texas, M.D. Anderson Cancer Center, Department of Biomathematics, Houston, TX.

Brun, Jorge M. and Thadis W. Box. 1963. Comparison of line intercepts and random point frames for sampling desert shrub vegetation. J. Range Management. 16:21-25.

Buckner, D.L. 1985. Point-intercept sampling in revegetation studies; maximizing objectivity and repeatability. Proceedings of the American Society of Surface Mining and Reclamation. 1985 Annual Meeting, Denver, CO.

Call, Mayo W. 1981. Terrestrial wildlife inventories - some methods and concepts. U.S. Dept. of the Interior, BLM Tech. Note No. 349. 171 p.

Canfield, R.H. 1941. Application of the line interception method in sampling range vegetation. J. Forestry 39:388-394.

———. 1944. Measurement of grazing use by the line intercept Method. Jour. For. 42(3):192-194.

Chambers Jeanne C., Ray W. Brown. 1983. Methods for Vegetation and Analysis on Revegetated Mined Lands. USDA, Forest Service General Technical Note INT-151. 57 p.

Clark, Ronnie. 1980. Erosion condition classification system. U.S. Dept. of the Interior, BLM Tech. Note No. 346. 47 p.

Cochran, William G. 1977. Sampling Techniques. John Wiley & Sons, Inc. New York, NY.

Cohen, J. 1988. Statistical power analysis for the behavioral sciences. Lawrence Erlbaum Associates, Hillsdale, NJ.

Cook, C. Wayne and James Stubbendieck. 1986. Range Research: Basic Problems and Techniques. Society for Range Management. Denver, CO.

## REFERENCES

Crocker, R.L. and N.S. Tiver. 1948. Survey methods in grassland ecology. Journal of the British Grassland Society 3: 1-26.

Cuplin, Paul. 1978. The use of large scale color infrared photography for stream habitat inventory. U.S. Dept. of the Interior, BLM Tech. Note No. 325. 11 p.

Daubenmire, Rexford. 1959. A Canopy-coverage method of vegetational analysis. Northwest Science 33:43-64.

———. 1968. Plant communities: a textbook of plant synecology. Harper and Row, New York. 300 p.

Dawson, Bruce E. 1981. Relative effectiveness of true-color, color infrared, black and white infrared and red-band sensitive films in identification of plant species. M.S. Thesis. Humboldt St. Univ., Arcata, CA. 101 p.

Dayton, W.A. 1950. Glossary of Botanical Terms Commonly Used in Range Research, USDA Miscellaneous Publication No 110, 40 p.

Despain, D.W., P.R. Ogden, and E.L. Smith. 1991. Plant frequency sampling for monitoring rangelands. In: G.B. Ruyle, ed. Some Methods for Monitoring Rangelands and other Natural Area Vegetation. Extension Report 9043, University of Arizona, College of Agriculture, Tucson, AZ.

DeVries, P.G. 1979. Line intersect sampling-statistical theory, applications, and suggestions for extended use in ecological inventory. In: R.M. Cormack, G.P. Patil and D.S. Robson, eds., Sampling Biological Populations, Vol. 5: Statistical Ecology, pp. 1-70. International Cooperative Publishing House, Fairland, MD.

Dixon, W.J., and F.J. Massey, Jr. 1983. Introduction to statistical analysis, 4th ed. McGraw-Hill, New York, NY.

Duncan, Don A. and Robert G. Woodmansee. 1975. Forecasting forage yield from precipitation in California's annual rangeland. J. Range Manage. 28:327-329.

Eckert, Richard E., Jr. and John S. Spencer. 1986. Vegetation response on allotments grazed under rest rotation management. Soc. for Range Manage. 39 (2): 166-173.

Ellison, Lincoln, A.R. Croft, and Reed W. Bailey. 1951. Indicators of condition and trend on high range-watersheds of the Intermountain Region. U.S. Dept. of Agr., For. Ser., Agr. Handbook No. 19. 66 p.

Evans, Raymond A. and R. Merton Love. 1957. The step-point method of sampling a practical tool in range research. J. Range Manage. 10:208-212.

Everitt, J.H., A.H. Gerbermann, N.A. Alaniz, and R.L. Bowen. 1980. Using 70-mm aerial photography to identify rangeland sites. Photogrammetric Engineering and Remote Sensing 46:1339-1348.

Fisser, H.G. and G.M. Van Dyne. 1966. Influence of number and spacing of points on accuracy and precision of basal cover estimates. J. Range Manage. 19:205-211.

Floyd, D.A. and J.E. Anderson. 1983. A new point interception frame for estimating cover of vegetation. Idaho National Engineering Laboratory Radioecology and Ecology Programs 1983 Progress Report, pp. 107-113.

———. 1987. A comparison of three methods for estimating plant cover. Journal of Ecology 75: 229-245.

Francis, Richard E., Richard S. Driscoll, and Jack N. Reppert. 1972. Loop-frequency as related to plant cover, herbage production, and plant density. U.S. Dept. of Agr., For. Ser., Rocky Mtn. For. and Range Exp. Sta., Ft. Collins, CO. Research Paper MA-94. 15 p.

Freese, Frank. 1962. Elementary forest sampling. U.S. Dept. of Agr., For. Ser., Agr. Handbook No. 232. 91 p.

———. 1967. Elementary statistical methods for foresters. U.S. Dept. of Agr., For. Ser., Agr. Handbook No. 317. 87 p.

Goldstein, R. 1989. Power and sample size via MS/PC-DOS computers. American Statistician 43:253-260.

Goodall, D.W. 1952. Some considerations in the use of point quadrats for the analysis of vegetation. Aust. J. Sci. Res., Series B 5:1-41.

Greig-Smith, P. 1983. Quantitative plant ecology. 3rd Ed. University of California Press, Berkeley and Los Angeles, CA.

Hanley, Thomas A. 1978. A comparison of the line-interception and quadrat estimation methods of determining shrub canopy coverage. J. Range Manage. 31:60-62.

Hansen, Herbert C. 1962. Dictionary of ecology. Bonanza Books, Crown Publishers, Inc., New York. 382 p.

Harniss, Roy 0. and Robert B. Murray. 1976. Reducing bias in dry leaf weight estimates of big sagebrush. Jr. Range Manage. 29:430-432.

Hart, R.H. 1980. Determining a proper stocking rate for a grazing system. In: Proceedings, Grazing Management Systems for South West Rangelands Symposium, Range Improvement Task Force, New Mexico State Univ., Las Cruces, NM, pp.49-64.

Heady, Harold F. 1961. Continuous vs. specialized grazing systems: a review and application to the California annual type. J. Range Manage. 14:182-193.

Heintz, T.W., J.K. Lewis, and S.S. Waller. 1979. Low-level aerial photography as a management and research tool for range inventory. J. Range Manage. 32:247-249.

Hewitt, George B., Ellis W. Huddleston, Robert J. Lavigne, Darrell N. Ueckert, and J. Gordon Watts. 1974. Rangeland entomology. Society for Range Management, Range Science Series No. 2. 127 p.

## REFERENCES

Hironaka, M. 1985. Frequency approaches to monitor rangeland vegetation. Symp. on use of frequency and for rangeland monitoring. William C. Krueger, Chairman. Proc., 38th Annual Meeting, Soc. for Range Manag. Feb. 1985. Salt Lake City, UT. Soc. for Range Manage. 84-86.

Hyder, D.N., C.E. Conrad, P.T. Tueller, L.D. Calvin, C.E. Poulton, and F.A. Sneva. 1963. Frequency sampling of sagebrush-bunchgrass vegetation. Ecology 44:740-746.

Hyder, D.N., R.E. Bement, E.E. Remmenga, and C. Terwilliger, Jr. 1965. Frequency sampling of blue grama range. J. Range Manage. 18:94-98.

Hyder, D.N., R.E. Bement, and C. Terwilliger. 1966. Vegetation-soils and vegetation-grazing relations from frequency data. J. Range Manage. 19:11-17.

Jardine, J.T. and Forsling, C.L. 1922. Range and cattle management during drought. USDA Bul. 1031, 84 p.

Jasmer, Gerald E. and Jerry Holechek. 1984. Determining Grazing Intensity on Rangelands. Journal of Soil and Water Conservation. 39(1):32-35.

Jones, M.B. and R.A. Evans. 1959. Modification of the step-point method for evaluating species yield changes in fertilizer trials on annual grasslands. Agron. J. 51:467-470.

Kennedy, K.A. and P.A. Addison. 1987. Some considerations for the use of visual estimates of plant cover in biomonitoring. J. Ecology 75: 151-157.

Kinsinger, Floyd E., Richard E. Eckert, and Pat O. Currie. 1960. A comparison of the line-interception, variable-plot, and loop methods as used to measure shrub-crown cover. J. Range Manage. 13:17-21.

Krebs, C.J. 1989. Ecological methodology. Harper & Row, New York, NY.

Lapin, Lawrence L. 1993. Statistics for Modern Business Decisions. 6th Ed. Dryden Press, Orlando, FL. 1265p.

Laycock, W.A. 1987. Setting Objectives and Picking Appropriate Methods for Monitoring Vegetation on Rangelands. Rangeland Monitoring Workshop Proceedings. U.S. Department of Interior. Bureau of Land Management. Golden, CO.

Levy, E.B. and E.A. Madden. 1933. The Point Method for Pasture Analysis. New Zealand J. Agric. 46: 267-279.

Lillesand, Thomas M. and Ralph Kiefer. 1979. Remote sensing and image interpretation. John Wiley and Sons, New York, NY. 612 p.

Lucas, H.A. and G.A.F. Seber. 1977. Estimating coverage and particle density using the line intercept method. Biometricka 64:618-622.

Lund, H. Gyde and Elise McNutt. 1979. Integrating inventories: an annotated bibliography. U.S. Dept. of the Interior, BLM Tech Note No. 333. 183 p.

Mack, R. and D.A. Pyke. 1979. Mapping individual plants with a field portable digitizer. Ecology 60:459-461.

McDougald, Neil K. and Richard C. Platt. 1976. A method of determining utilization for wet mountain meadows on the Summit Allotment, Sequoia National Forest, California. J. Range Manage. 29:497-501.

McQuisten, Richard and Karl A. Gebhardt. 1983. Analytical reliability in the decision making process—the numbers game. J. Range Manage. 36:126-128.

Meyer, Merle, Fred Batson, and Duane Whitmer. 1982. Helicopter-borne 35mm aerial photography applications to range and riparian studies. IAFHE RSL Res. Rep. 82-1, Coll. of Forestry and Agricultural Experiment Station, Univ. of Minn., St. Paul, MN. 80 p.

Meyer, Merle and Phillip Grumstrup. 1978. Operating manual for the 35mm aerial photography system, 2nd Rev. IAFHE RSL Res. Rep. 78-1, Coll. of Forestry, Univ. of Minn., St. Paul, MN. 62 p.

Milne, A. 1959. The centric systematic area-sample treated as a random sample. Biometrics 15:270-297.

Morris, Meredith J. 1973. Estimating understory plant cover with rated microplots. U.S. Dept. of Agr., For. Ser., Rocky Mtn. For. and Range Exp. Sta., Ft. Collins, CO., Research Paper RM-104. 12 p.

Morrison, R.G. and G.A. Yarranton. 1970. An instrument for Rapid and Precise Point-sampling of Vegetation. Can. J. Bot. 48: 293-297.

Mueggler, W.F. 1976. Number of plots required for measuring productivity of mountain grasslands in Montana. U.S. Dept. of Agr., For. Ser., Res. Note INT-207. Intermountain For. and Range Exp. Sta., Ogden, UT. 6 p.

Mueller-Dombois, Dieter and Heinz Ellenberg. 1974. Aims and methods of vegetation ecology. John Wiley & Sons, New York, NY. 547p.

Murphy, Alfred H. 1970. Predicted forage yield based on fall precipitation in California annual grasslands. J. Range Manage. 23:363-365.

Myers, Wayne L. and Ronald L. Shelton. 1980. Survey methods for ecosystem management. A Wiley-Interscience Publication, John Wiley & Sons, New York, NY. 403 p.

National Academy of Sciences/National Research Council. 1962. Basic problems and techniques in range research. NAS/NRC Publ. 890. 341 p.

National Wildlife Federation. 1978. Application of remote sensing data to wildlife management. Sioux Falls, S.D., Pecora IV, Proceedings of the Symposium, National Wildlife Federation Scientific and Tech. Series 3. 397 p.

Nevada Range Studies Task Group. 1984. Nevada Rangeland Monitoring Handbook. Bureau of Land Management Nevada State Office, Reno, NV. 50p.

## REFERENCES

Nie, Norman H., C. Hadlai Hull, Jean G. Jenkins, Karin Steinbrenner, and Dale H. Bent. 1975. Statistical package for the social sciences, SPSS. 2nd Ed. McGraw-Hill Book Co., New York, NY. 675 p.

Nudds, Thomas D. 1977. Quantifying the vegetative structure of wildlife cover. Wildlife Society Bulletin 5:113-117.

Odum, Eugene P. 1971. Fundamentals of ecology. 3rd Ed. W.B. Saunders Co., Philadelphia, PA. 547 p.

Oosting, Henry J. 1956. The study of plant communities - an introduction to plant ecology. 2nd Ed. W.H. Freeman and Co., San Francisco, CA. 440 p.

Parker, Kenneth. 1954. Application of ecology in the determination of range condition and trend. J. Range Manage. 7:14-24.

Payne, G.F. 1974. Cover-weight relationships. J. Range Manage. 27:403-404.

Pechanec, J.F. and G.D. Pickford. 1937. A weight-estimate method for the determination of range or pasture production. J. Amer. Soc. Agron. 29:894-904.

Pechanec, J.F. and George Stewart. 1949. Grazing spring-fall sheep ranges of southern Idaho. U.S. Dept. of Agr., Circular No. 808. 34 p.

Phillips, E.A. 1959. Methods of vegetation study. Holt, Rinehart, and Winston, Inc., New York, NY. 107 p.

Pieper, Rex D. 1973. Measurement techniques for herbaceous and shrubby vegetation. Dept. of Animal and Range Sciences, New Mexico State Univ., Las Cruces, NM. 149 p.

Pierce, W.R. and L.E. Eddleman. 1970. A field stereographic technique for range analysis. J. Range Manage. 23:218-220.

Pitt, Michael D. and Harold F. Heady. 1979. The effects of grazing intensity on annual vegetation. J. Range Manage. 32:109-114.

Reppert, Jack N. and Richard E. Francis. 1973. Interpretation of trend in range condition from 3-step data. U.S. Dept. of Agr., For. Ser., Rocky Mtn. For. and Range Exp. Sta., Ft. Collins, CO., Research Paper RM-103. 15 p.

Richardson, Arlo E. 1981. Report on the feasibility of using phenoclimatography models to predict range development and production on BLM winter ranges. BLM Contract No. UT-910-CTO-003. 73 p.

Richardson, Arlo E. and Stephen G. Leonard. 1981. Climatic modeling of winter rangelands in Utah. In: Ext. Abstract 15th Conf. on Agr. and For. Meteorology and 5th Conf. on biometeorology, Anaheim, CA. p. 182-185.

Riser, Paul G. 1984. Methods for Inventory and Monitoring of Vegetation, Litter, and Soil Surface Condition. Developing Strategies for Rangeland Monitoring. National Research Council National Academy of Sciences.

Robel, R.J., J.N. Briggs, A.D. Dayton, and L.C. Hulbert. 1970. Relationships Between Visual Obstruction Measurements and Weight of Grassland Vegetation, J. Range Manage. 23:295.

Robel, R.J. 1970. Possible Role of Behavior in Regulating Greater Prairie Chickens' Populations, J. Wildlife Manage. Vol 34:306-312.

Rossiter, R.C. 1966. Ecology of the Mediterranean annual-type pasture. Advances in Agronomy 18:1-56.

Salzer, D. 1994. An introduction to sampling and sampling design for vegetation monitoring. Unpublished papers prepared for Bureau of Land Management Training Course 1730-5. BLM Training Center, Phoenix, AZ.

Sampson, Arthur W. 1952. Range management - principles and practices. John Wiley and Sons, New York, NY. 570 p.

Schaeffer, R.L., W. Mendenhall, and L. Ott. 1979. Elementary survey sampling. Duxbury Press, North Scituate, MA.

Schmutz, Ervin M. 1978. Let's put manage in range management. Rangeman's Journal 5:185-188.

Schultz, Arnold M., Robert P. Gibbens, and Leonard DeBano. 1961. Artificial populations for teaching and testing range techniques. J. Range Manage. 14:236-242.

Schwartz, Chas. C., Edward C. Thor, and Gary H. Elsner. 1976. Wildlands planning glossary. U.S. Dept. of Agr., For. Ser., Pacific Southwest For. and Range Exp. Sta., Berkeley, Calif., Gen. Tech. Rept. PSW-13. 252 p.

Seher, J. Scott and Paul T. Tueller. 1973. Color aerial photos for marshland. Photogrammetric Engineering 39:489-499.

Smith, A.D. 1944. A study of the reliability of range vegetation estimates. Ecology 25:441-448.

———. 1965. Determining common use grazing capacities by application of the key species concept. J. Range Manage. 18:196-201.

Smith, J.G. 1959. Additional modifications of the point frame. J. Range Manage. 12:204-205.

Smith, Stuart D. 1982. Evaluation of the frequency plot method as an improved technique for measuring successional trend. M.S. Thesis. Univ. of Idaho, Moscow, ID. 95 p.

Snedecor, George W. and William C. Cochran. 1974. Statistical methods. Iowa State University Press, Ames, IA. 573 p.

Snyder, W.D. 1991. Wheat stubble as nesting cover for ring necked pheasants in northern Colorado. Wildlife Soc. Bulletin vol 19:4.

Society for Range Management. 1974. A glossary of terms used in range management. 2nd Ed. M.M. Kothmann (ed.), SN4 Publ. 36 p.

————. 1975. Rangeland reference areas. William A. Laycock (ed.), SN4 Publ , Range Science Series, No. 3. 66 p.

————. 1983. Guidelines and terminology for range inventories and monitoring. Report of the Range Inventory Standardization Committee. 13 p.

————. 1985. Proceedings of Special Symposium - Rangeland Monitoring.

Spalinger, D.E. 1980. Vegetation Changes on Eight Selected Deer Ranges in Nevada Over a 15-Year Period. Nevada State Office Bureau of Land Management.

Stanton, F.W. 1960. Ocular Point Frame. J. Range Manage. 13:153.

Steel, Robert G.D. and James H. Torrie. 1980. 2nd Ed. Principles and procedures of statistics. McGraw-Hill Book Co., New York, NY. 633 p.

Stoddart, Laurence A., Arthur D. Smith, and Thadis W. Box. 1975. Range management. 3rd Ed. McGraw-Hill Book Co., New York. 532 p.

Tueller, Paul T. 1977. Large scale 70mm photography for range resources analysis in the western United States. In: Proc. 11th Int'l. Symp. on Remote Sensing, Ann Arbor, MI. pp. 1507-1514.

————. 1979. Some aspects of the use of dichotomous keys to aid in the interpretation of color aerial photographs for vegetation mapping. In: Proc. ASP 7th Annual Workshop on Color Aerial Photography in the Plant Sciences, Davis, CA. pp. 189-200.

————. 1988. Vegetation Science Applications for Rangeland Analysis and Management. Kluwer Academic Publishers, Boston, MA. 642 p.

Tueller, Paul T., Garwin Lorain, Karl Kipping, and Charles Wilkie. 1972. Methods for measuring vegetation changes on Nevada rangelands. Agr. Exp. Sta., Univ. of Nevada, Reno, NV. T16. 55 p.

Tueller, Paul T. and D. Terry Booth. 1974. Photographic remote sensing techniques for erosion on wildlands. BLM Contract 08550-CTS-2, Coll. of Agr., Univ. of Nevada, Reno, NV. 97 p.

Uresk, D.W., R.O. Gilbert, and W.H. Rickard. 1977. Sampling big sagebrush for phytomass. J. Range Manage. 30:311-314.

USDA, Forest Service. 1959. Techniques and methods of measuring understory vegetation. Proc. of Symp. at Tifton, Georgia, Oct. 1958. U.S. Dept. of Agr., For. Ser., Southern For. Exp. Sta. and Southeastern For. Exp. Sta. 174 p.

————. 1963. Range research methods. Proc. of Symp., Denver, CO, May 1962. U.S. Dept. of Agr., Misc. Publ. No. 940. 172 p.

———. 1981. Arid land resource inventories: developing cost-efficient methods. U.S. Dept. of Agr., For. Ser., Gen. Tech. Rep. WO-28. 620 p.

———. 1962. Range Research Methods - a Symposium. USDA Forest Service, Misc Publ. 940, Denver, CO.

———. 1994. Rangeland Analysis and Management Training Guide, Rocky Mountain Region USDA Forest Service Denver, CO.

USDA, Soil Conservation Service. 1976. National Range Handbook. 154 p.

U.S. Department of Interior, Bureau of Land Management, Vegetation Attributes Reference Card. BLM Phoenix Training Center.

———. 1982. Big Game Studies, BLM Manual 6630.

———. 1983. Inventory and Monitoring Coordination, BLM Manual 1734.

———. 1984 (rev. 1990). National Range Handbook 4410-1. Washington, D.C.

———. 1984. Rangeland Monitoring: Planning for Monitoring, TR4400-1.

———. 1985. Rangeland Monitoring - Trend Studies, TR4400-4.

———. 1987. Riparian Inventory and Monitoring, Montana BLM Riparian Tech. Bull. No.1.

———. 1993. Rangeland Monitoring - Supplemental Studies, TR4400-5.

USDI, Fish & Wildlife Service. 1981. Estimating wildlife habitat variables. FWS/OBS - 81/47. 111 p.

Van Dyne, George M. 1960. A procedure for rapid collection, processing, and analysis of line intercept data. J. Range Manage. 13:247-251.

Van Dyne, George M., W.G. Vogel, and H.G. Fisser. 1963. Influence of small plot size and shape on range herbage production estimates. Ecology 44:746-759.

Waller, S.S., J.K. Lewis, M.A. Brown, T.W. Heintz, R.I. Butterfield, and F.R. Gartner. 1978. Use of 35mm aerial photography in vegetation sampling. In: Proceedings, First International Rangeland Congress. Hyder, D.N. (ed), Soc. for Range Manage., Denver, CO. pp. 517-520.

Wells, K.F. 1971. Measuring vegetation changes on fixed quadrats by vertical ground stereophotography. J. Range Manage. 24:233-236.

West, N.E. 1985. Shortcomings of plant frequency-based methods for range condition and trend. William C. Krueger, Chairman. Proc., 38th Annual Meeting Soc. for Range Manage. Feb. 1985. Salt Lake City. Soc. for Range Manage. 87-90.

## REFERENCES

Whitman, W.C. and E.I. Siggeirsson. 1954. Comparison of line interception and point contact methods in the analysis of mixed range vegetation. Ecology 35:431-436.

Whysong, G.L. and W.W. Brady, 1987. Frequency Sampling and Type II Errors, J. Range Manage. 40:172-174.

Wiegert, R.G. 1962. The selection of an optimum quadrat size for sampling the standing crop of grasses and forbs. Ecology 43:125-129.

Williams, B. 1978. A sampler on sampling. John Wiley & Sons, New York, NY.

Willoughby, John W. 1993. Sampling and analysis problems associated with Bureau of Land Management Technical Reference 4400-4 (Trend Studies), Personal Information Memorandum.

Wilm, H.G., D.F. Costello, and G.E. Klipple. 1944. Estimating forage yield by the double-sampling method. Amer. Soc. Agron. J. 36:194-203.

Winkworth, R.E., R.A. Perry, and C.V. Rossetti. 1962. A comparison of methods of estimating plant cover in an arid grassland community. J. Range Manage. 15:194-196.

Winkworth, R.E. and D.W. Goodall. 1962. A Crosswire Sighting Tube for Point-Quadrat Analysis. Ecology 43:342-343.

Wright, Henry A. 1967. Contrasting responses of squirreltail and needle-and-thread to herbage removal. J. Range Manage. 20:398-400.

Zar, Jerrold H. 1984. Biostatistical analysis, 2nd Ed. Prentice-Hall, Inc., Englewood Cliffs, NJ. 718 p.

# APPENDIX A

# Study Location and Documentation Data Form

## Study Location & Documentation Data

| Study Method | | Study Number |
|---|---|---|

| Allotment Name & Number | Pasture |
|---|---|

| District | Resource Area |
|---|---|

| Ecological Site | Plant Community |
|---|---|

| Date Established | Established by (Name) | Map Reference |
|---|---|---|

| Elevation | Slope | Exposure | Aerial Photo Reference |
|---|---|---|---|

| Township | Range | Section | 1/4 | 1/4 | 1/4 |
|---|---|---|---|---|---|

Location

Scale: ____ inches equals one mile

| Key Species | | | | | |
|---|---|---|---|---|---|
| | | | | | |
| 1          2          3 | | | | | |

| Distance and bearing between reference post or reference point and the transect location stake, beginning of transect, or plot | | | | | |
|---|---|---|---|---|---|
| | | | | | |

Distance and bearing between location stake and bearing stake

| Transect Bearing | Vertical Distance Between Ground & Aligned Tape |
|---|---|

| Length of Transect | Plot/Frame Size |
|---|---|

| Sampling Interval | Total Number of Samples |
|---|---|

Notes (Description of study location, diagram of transect/plot layout, description of photo points, etc. If more space is needed, use reverse side or another page.)

Note:   Depending on the study method, fill in the blocks that apply when a study is established. This documentation enables the examiners to conduct follow-up studies in a consistant manner to provide comparable data for analysis, interpretation, and evaluation.

## Study Location & Documentation Data

Study Method _Daubenmire Trend_

Study Number
_035-27W-08-03_

Allotment Name & Number _Quaking Aspen -11037_

Pasture _Sheep Creek_

District _Howe_

Resource Area _Lost Mountain_

Ecological Site _Clayey -15-19" Northern Plains_

Plant Community _ARTR 2 - AGSP - PONE 3_

Date Established
_7/24/84_

Established by (Name)
_Charlie Wagon_

Map Reference
_Graystone 7½ min. topo._

Elevation _4300_

Slope _Flat_

Exposure _East_

Aerial Photo Reference
_BLM-24CN-A277A - 4/22/78_

| | Township | Range | Section | 1/4 | 1/4 | 1/4 | |
|---|---|---|---|---|---|---|---|
| Location | 3 S | 27 W | 8 | NW | SE | NW | Scale: _2_ inches equals one mile |

Key Species

| | | | | |
|---|---|---|---|---|
| | | | X | |

1 _AGSP_        2 _PONE 3_        3

Distance and bearing between reference post or reference point and the transect location stake, beginning of transect, or plot

_The transect location stake is 100 ft. south (180°) of the reference post. Reference post is 3 miles west of Redtop Reservoir._

Distance and bearing between location stake and bearing stake _122 feet at 135°_

Transect Bearing

Vertical Distance Between Ground & Aligned Tape
_3 inches_

Length of Transect _100 Feet_

Plot/Frame Size _20x50 cm - 6 cover classes_

Sampling Interval _Every 2 ft. beginnig at the 1-foot mark on the tape. Place the rear left corner of the frame at every 2nd foot mark along the right side of the tape._

Total Number of Samples _50_

Notes (Description of study location, diagram of transect/plot layout, description of photo points, etc. If more space is needed, use reverse side or another page.)

_The two photo plots are located at 37 and 53 feet along the tape. Close-up photos are taken from the northeast side of the photo plots._

Note: Depending on the study method, fill in the blocks that apply when a study is established. This documentation enables the examiners to conduct follow-up studies in a consistant manner to provide comparable data for analysis, interpretation, and evaluation.

# APPENDIX B—STUDY AND PHOTOGRAPH IDENTIFICATION

A. **Numbering Studies** Studies should be numbered to assure positive identification. These numbers can also be used to identify photographs. Following are three alternative schemes for numbering studies:

1. *Numbering Scheme 1.* Consecutive numbers may be assigned to studies within an allotment. For example, Mooncreek #1 and Mooncreek #2 would be studies Number 1 and 2 within the Mooncreek Allotment. A disadvantage to using the names of allotments in a numbering scheme is that these names can, and often do, change.

2. *Numbering Scheme 2.* Studies may be numbered based on their location within a township, range, and section. A 10-character number can be assigned in the following manner:

   a The first three characters are the township (03S), the second three are the range (27W), the next two are the section (08), and the last two are simply a series number (01) assigned to a study based on the number of studies located within a section.

   b The numbers for studies located in Section 8 would be 03S-27W-08-01, 03S-27W-08-02, and so forth.

   c Depending on the local situation, this scheme can be modified by adding characters to the code where there are fractional townships or ranges, where there are more than 99 sections/tracts within a township, and/or where there is more than one public land survey principal meridian and baseline within the area of jurisdiction.

3. *Numbering Scheme 3.* Studies may be numbered based on their location relative to the initial point of survey (principal meridian and baseline governing public land survey).

   a Under this scheme, the first character is a letter assigned to a principal meridian and baseline quadrant. Using the initial point of the survey as the center point, the northeast quadrant (townships located to the north and east of the initial point) is coded "A". The northwest, southwest, and southeast quadrants are coded "B", "C", and "D", respectively. For example:

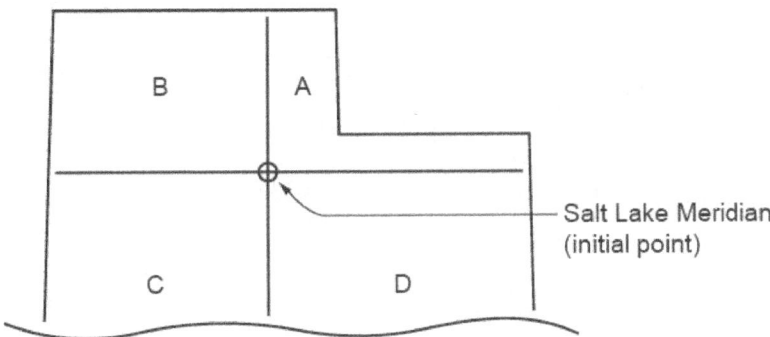

b The next characters are the township number (3, 16, etc.) followed by the range number (7, 32, etc.) and the section number (8, 21, etc.).

c The next three characters are used to identify the subdivisions within a section (down to 10 acres) in which a study is located. These subdivisions have letter designations as follows:

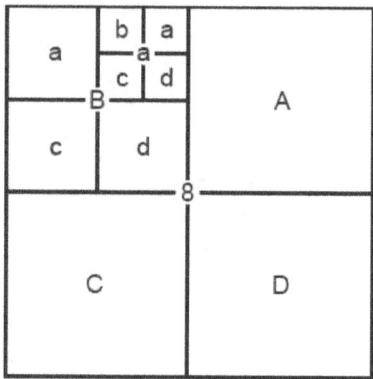

d The last character(s) is (are) simply a series number (1, 2, 3, . . . 10, 11, etc.) assigned to a study based on the number of studies located within the smallest subdivision.

e For example, Studies 1 and 2 located in the SE1/4NE1/4NW1/4 of Section 8, T3S, R21E would be numbered (D-3-21)8Bad-1 and (D-3-21)8Bad-2.

f Depending on the local situation, this scheme can be modified by adding characters to the code where there are fractional townships or ranges, where there are more than 99 sections/tracts within a township, and/or where there is more than one public land survey principal meridian and baseline within the area of jurisdiction.

## B. Identifying Photographs

In most cases, the number that has been assigned to a study is the number used to identify the photographs associated with that study. Following is a description of three labels that can be used to include the study number in the photographs:

1. *Label 1* The Photo Identification Label included as Appendix C can be copied and used to identify photographs. This label provides space for documenting the date, number, and location (Resource Area, allotment, and pasture) of a study. A large black felt-tip marking pen should be used to print the information on the label.

2. *Label 2* A slotted sign board with a black felt background and movable white plastic letters can be used as a photo identification label. Room permitting, the user may include any information desired on such a label. A 9- x 12-inch board with slots running lengthwise at a spacing of 1/4-inch and 1-1/2-inch white letters makes a highly visible label for most photographs.

3. *Label 3* A placard on which identifying characteristics can be entered can be developed to meet local field needs. The placard can be constructed of heavy white cardboard on which such things as Date, "T" (township), "R" (range), Section Number, etc., are preprinted. A heavy mylar film can be placed over the preprinted placard. The specific identifying information can be handprinted on the mylar with a heavy grease pencil or other readily removable, highly visible, marking material. After taking the desired photographs, the mylar can be wiped clean and the placard reused for other photographs. A more permanent placard can be constructed of plywood and painted enamel white. The grease pencil markings can be wiped from the enameled surface and the placard reused for other photographs. Caution must be exercised in the placement of the placard to prevent glare from the mylar or enameled surface.

NOTE - Labels can be placed flat on the ground immediately adjacent to photo plots for close-up photographs.

- Labels can be placed in an upright position in the foreground of general view photographs.

# APPENDIX C

## Photo Identification Label

DATE

NO.

R.A.

ALLOT.

PAST.

DATE 7/24/84

NO. 035-27W-08-03

R.A. *Lost Mountain*

ALLOT. *Quaking Aspen*

PAST. *Sheep Creek*

# APPENDIX D—
# SELECTING RANDOM SAMPLES

Selecting random points along a baseline from which to run transects:

1. *Select Direction*  If the baseline bisects the middle of the sample area, the first determination for selecting the location of a transect is to determine the direction each transect will be run perpendicular to the baseline. A simple flip of a coin could be used. Another way of selecting directions is to arbitrarily decide that odd numbers represent transects to the right of the baseline and even numbers represent transects to the left of the baseline. If five transects are required along a 100-meter baseline, start at some arbitrary point anywhere on the random digit table below and select the first five single digit numbers from left to right. As an example, the process could begin with the number sequence in row 15, column 4 (22695). Transects 1, 2, and 3 would be run to the left (numbers 2, 2, and 6), and transects 4 and 5 would be run to the right (9 and 5).

2. *Select Location*  To select the location of each transect along the baseline, again start at some arbitrary point on the table of random numbers. In this case, use two-digit sequences. If row 19, column 3, is selected as the starting point, the five two-digit sequences would be 33, 52, 15, 56, and 37. Transects would be run at the 15-, 33-, 37-, 52-, and 56- meter marks along the baseline. Care should be taken to ensure that adjoining transects do not overlap. Depending on the ecological site and vegetation community, any interval can be selected as the minimum distance between transects. In this case, 10 meters has been established as the distance between transects. In the above example, the second and third transects (at the 33- and 37-meter marks) are within 10 meters of each other on the same side of the baseline. If they were to be run in opposite directions, there would be no problem. Since they are to be run in the same direction, discard the transect at the 37-meter mark and select the next two-digit sequence. A transect at the 39-meter mark (the next two digits in the table) is still within 10 meters of the previous transect. Continue the process until all transects are separated by 10 meters. With the next two-digit number sequence being 78, transect locations are now at the 15-, 33-, 52-, 56-, and 78- meter marks. Since the new third and fourth transects (52 and 56) are in opposite directions, the five transect locations have been determined.

The table of random numbers could also be used for baselines over 100 meters. If the baseline is 200 meters, use a three-digit sequence to select the location of each transect. Only those three-digit numbers that fall between 1 and 200 would be used. This method requires the selection of many numbers because most will not fall between 1 and 200.

There is a more efficient method of selecting random samples, particularly for two-, three-, and higher-digit numbers. To use this method, the random numbers must be treated as decimals. In our set of random digits, we would simply place a decimal point in front of every group of five digits and treat each group as one random number. Thus, if we entered the table at row 26, column 7, and read across, we would have the following six random numbers: 0.32978, 0.59902, 0.05463, 0.09245, 0.37631, and 0.74016. If we used a random number generator, it would be even easier since these provide random numbers as decimals falling between 0 and 1.

The formula for using these decimal random numbers for selecting a sampling unit or point is:

$$[u \times N] + 1$$

Where:  u = random number (expressed as decimal)
N = total population size
[ ] = used to indicate that only the integer part of the product is used in the calculation

To illustrate how this formula works, let's say that our baseline is 200 meters long. Here we need to select numbers between 0 and 200 as points along a baseline. Consider these points as a "population" of 200 possible points. Using the first of the six random numbers we came up with above, 0.32978, we calculate:

$$[0.32978 \times 200] + 1$$
$$= [65.956] + 1$$
$$= 65 + 1$$
$$= 66$$

Thus, 66 is the first point. Using the second random number we have:

$$[0.59902 \times 200] + 1$$
$$= [119.80400] + 1$$
$$= 119 + 1$$
$$= 120$$

Now we have the second point, 120. We continue in this manner until we have the five points we need. Although the formula may look difficult, a hand-held calculator or computer program with a random number generator makes it easy.

The reason for adding the 1 to the integer of the product of the random number and N is that only whole numbers will be used. Without adding 1, it would be impossible to obtain the number 200. Consider the highest possible random number we could obtain, 0.99999. If we multiply this number by 200, we obtain 199.99800; taking the whole integer of this number yields the number 199. Adding 1 makes it 200.

As a rule of thumb, you should make sure the random numbers have more digits on the right side of the decimal point than the number of digits in N. In the example above, N is 200 and we are using random numbers with five digits to the right of the decimal point, so we are okay.

Note that this process is much more efficient than the first method because we do not need to reject any numbers. Given the fact that there is only a 1 in 5 chance of any three-digit number falling between 1 and 200, we would—on the average—have to examine 25 three-digit numbers to come up with five points under the first method. Using the second method, on the other hand, we can use the first five random numbers from the table to select the same five points.

## Table of Random Digits (Zar 1984)

| | 00-04 | 05-09 | 10-14 | 15-19 | 20-24 | 25-29 | 30-34 | 35-39 | 40-44 | 45-49 |
|---|---|---|---|---|---|---|---|---|---|---|
| 00 | 22808 | 04391 | 45529 | 53968 | 57136 | 98228 | 85485 | 13801 | 68194 | 56382 |
| 01 | 49305 | 36965 | 44849 | 64987 | 59501 | 35141 | 50159 | 57369 | 76913 | 75739 |
| 02 | 81934 | 19920 | 73316 | 69243 | 69605 | 17022 | 53264 | 83417 | 55193 | 92929 |
| 03 | 10840 | 13508 | 48120 | 22467 | 54505 | 70536 | 91206 | 81038 | 22418 | 34800 |
| 04 | 99555 | 73289 | 59605 | 37105 | 24621 | 44100 | 72832 | 12268 | 97089 | 68112 |
| 05 | 32677 | 45709 | 62337 | 35132 | 45128 | 96761 | 08745 | 53388 | 98353 | 46724 |
| 06 | 09401 | 75407 | 27704 | 11569 | 52842 | 83543 | 44750 | 03177 | 50511 | 15301 |
| 07 | 73424 | 31711 | 65519 | 74069 | 56744 | 40864 | 75315 | 89066 | 96563 | 75142 |
| 08 | 37075 | 81378 | 59472 | 71858 | 86903 | 66860 | 03757 | 32723 | 54273 | 45477 |
| 09 | 02060 | 37158 | 55244 | 44812 | 45369 | 78939 | 08048 | 28036 | 40946 | 03898 |
| 10 | 94719 | 43565 | 40028 | 79866 | 43137 | 28063 | 52513 | 66405 | 71511 | 66135 |
| 11 | 70234 | 48272 | 59621 | 88778 | 16536 | 36505 | 41724 | 24776 | 63971 | 01685 |
| 12 | 07972 | 71752 | 92745 | 86465 | 01845 | 27416 | 50519 | 48458 | 68460 | 63113 |
| 13 | 58521 | 64882 | 26993 | 48104 | 61307 | 73933 | 17214 | 44827 | 88306 | 78177 |
| 14 | 32580 | 45202 | 21148 | 09684 | 39411 | 04892 | 02055 | 75276 | 51831 | 85686 |
| 15 | 88796 | 30829 | 35009 | 22695 | 23694 | 11220 | 71006 | 26720 | 39476 | 60538 |
| 16 | 31525 | 82746 | 78935 | 82980 | 61236 | 28940 | 96341 | 13790 | 66247 | 33839 |
| 17 | 02747 | 35989 | 70387 | 89571 | 34570 | 17002 | 79223 | 96817 | 31681 | 15207 |
| 18 | 46651 | 28987 | 20525 | 61347 | 63981 | 41085 | 67412 | 29053 | 00724 | 14841 |
| 19 | 43598 | 14436 | 33521 | 55637 | 39789 | 26560 | 66404 | 71802 | 18763 | 80560 |
| 20 | 30596 | 92319 | 11474 | 64546 | 60030 | 73795 | 60809 | 24016 | 29166 | 36059 |
| 21 | 56198 | 64370 | 85771 | 62633 | 78240 | 05766 | 32419 | 35769 | 14057 | 80674 |
| 22 | 68266 | 67544 | 06464 | 84956 | 18431 | 04015 | 89049 | 15098 | 12018 | 89338 |
| 23 | 31107 | 28597 | 65102 | 75599 | 17496 | 87590 | 68848 | 33021 | 69855 | 54015 |
| 24 | 37555 | 05069 | 38680 | 87274 | 55152 | 21792 | 77219 | 48732 | 03377 | 01160 |
| 25 | 90463 | 27249 | 43845 | 94391 | 12145 | 36882 | 48906 | 52336 | 00780 | 74407 |
| 26 | 99189 | 88731 | 93531 | 52638 | 54989 | 04237 | 32978 | 59902 | 05463 | 09245 |
| 27 | 37631 | 74016 | 89072 | 59598 | 55356 | 27346 | 80856 | 80875 | 52850 | 36548 |
| 28 | 73829 | 21651 | 50141 | 76142 | 72303 | 06694 | 61697 | 76662 | 23745 | 96282 |
| 29 | 15634 | 89428 | 47090 | 12094 | 42134 | 62301 | 87236 | 90110 | 53463 | 46969 |
| 30 | 00571 | 45172 | 78532 | 63863 | 98597 | 15742 | 41967 | 11821 | 91389 | 07476 |
| 31 | 83374 | 10184 | 56384 | 27050 | 77700 | 13875 | 96607 | 76479 | 80535 | 17454 |
| 32 | 78666 | 85645 | 13181 | 08700 | 08289 | 62956 | 54439 | 39150 | 95690 | 18555 |
| 33 | 47890 | 88197 | 21358 | 65254 | 35917 | 54035 | 83028 | 84636 | 38186 | 50581 |
| 34 | 56238 | 13559 | 79344 | 83198 | 94542 | 35165 | 40188 | 21456 | 67024 | 62771 |
| 35 | 35369 | 32234 | 38129 | 59963 | 99237 | 72648 | 66504 | 99065 | 61161 | 16186 |
| 36 | 42934 | 34578 | 28968 | 74028 | 42164 | 55647 | 76805 | 61023 | 33099 | 48293 |
| 37 | 09010 | 15226 | 43474 | 30174 | 26727 | 39317 | 48508 | 55438 | 85336 | 40762 |
| 38 | 83897 | 90073 | 72941 | 85613 | 85569 | 24183 | 08247 | 15946 | 02957 | 68504 |
| 39 | 82206 | 01230 | 93252 | 89045 | 25141 | 91943 | 75531 | 87420 | 99012 | 80751 |
| 40 | 14175 | 32992 | 49046 | 41272 | 94040 | 44929 | 98531 | 27712 | 05106 | 35242 |
| 41 | 58968 | 88367 | 70927 | 74765 | 18635 | 85122 | 27722 | 95388 | 61523 | 91745 |
| 42 | 62601 | 04595 | 76926 | 11007 | 67631 | 64641 | 07994 | 04639 | 39314 | 83126 |
| 43 | 97030 | 71165 | 47032 | 85021 | 65554 | 66774 | 21560 | 04121 | 57297 | 85415 |
| 44 | 89074 | 31587 | 21360 | 41673 | 71192 | 85795 | 82157 | 52928 | 62586 | 02179 |
| 45 | 07806 | 81312 | 81215 | 99858 | 26762 | 28993 | 74951 | 64680 | 50934 | 32011 |
| 46 | 91540 | 86466 | 13229 | 76624 | 44092 | 96604 | 08590 | 89705 | 03424 | 48033 |
| 47 | 99279 | 27334 | 33804 | 77988 | 93592 | 90708 | 56780 | 70097 | 39907 | 51006 |
| 48 | 63224 | 05074 | 83941 | 25034 | 43516 | 22840 | 35230 | 66048 | 80754 | 46302 |
| 49 | 98351 | 97513 | 27529 | 65419 | 35328 | 19738 | 82366 | 38573 | 50967 | 72754 |

# REPORT DOCUMENTATION PAGE

Public reporting burden for this collection of information is estimated to average 1 hour per response, including the time for reviewing instructions, searching existing data sources, gathering and maintaining the data needed, and completing and reviewing the collection of information. Send comments regarding this burden estimate or any other aspect of this collection of information, including suggestions for reducing this burden, to Washington Headquarters Services, Directorate for Information Operations and Reports, 1215 Jefferson Davis Highway, Suite 1204, Arlington, VA 22202-4302, and to the Office of Management and Budget, Paperwork Reduction Project (0704-0188), Washington, DC 20503.

| 1. AGENCY USE ONLY (Leave blank) | 2. REPORT DATE<br>June 1996 | 3. REPORT TYPE AND DATES COVERED<br>Final |
|---|---|---|

**4. TITLE AND SUBTITLE**

Sampling Vegetation Attributes

**5. FUNDING NUMBERS**

**6. AUTHOR(S)**

Interagency Technical Team

**7. PERFORMING ORGANIZATION NAME(S) AND ADDRESS(ES)**

U.S. Department of the Interior
Bureau of Land Management - National Applied Resource Sciences Center
P.O. Box 25047
Denver, CO  80225-0047

**8. PERFORMING ORGANIZATION REPORT NUMBER**

BLM/RS/ST-96/002+1730

**9. SPONSORING/MONITORING AGENCY NAME(S) AND ADDRESS(ES)**

**10. SPONSORING/MONITORING AGENCY REPORT NUMBER**

**11. SUPPLEMENTARY NOTES**

**12a. DISTRIBUTION/AVAILABILITY STATEMENT**

**12b. DISTRIBUTION CODE**

**13. ABSTRACT** (Maximum 200 words)

This interagency technical reference provides the basis for consistent, uniform, and standard vegetation attribute sampling that is economical, repeatable, statistically reliable, and technically adequate. While not all inclusive, this reference does include the primary vegetation sampling methods used across the West (frequency methods, dry weight rank method, Daubenmire, line intercept, density method, comparative yield, etc.).

**14. SUBJECT TERMS**

- Rangeland inventory
- Rangeland monitoring
- Rangeland evaluation
- Vegetation attributes
- Vegetation sampling

**15. NUMBER OF PAGES**

176, including covers

**16. PRICE CODE**

| 17. SECURITY CLASSIFICATION OF REPORT<br>Unclassified | 18. SECURITY CLASSIFICATION OF THIS PAGE<br>Unclassified | 19. SECURITY CLASSIFICATION OF ABSTRACT<br>Unclassified | 20. LIMITATION OF ABSTRACT<br>UL |
|---|---|---|---|